From the Napoleonic Wars to the Devil's Device: The History of Weymouth and Its Neighbours, Volume II

AA COLLIER

ISBN-13: 978-0-9576282-2-9

DEDICATION

This is dedicated to Hannah who is an amazing editor and spends much of her time on the harbour.

Contents:

Images

To The Right Was Weymouth Itself, A Very Pretty Town...

Weymouth had begun to catch on as a sea-bathing resort by the 1760s and when the Duke of Gloucester built a house on the sea front after "discovering" the town, the national spotlight began to shine on the town. But it was really the Duke's brother King George III's adoption of the community as a favourite holiday destination that put it on the map as a resort for Britain's rich and famous.

The timing was perfect; Weymouth's harbour had been silting up over the previous hundred years, making it impossible for the bigger and better ships of the late 18th century to land at the ancient port town. That had turned the area into *a mere fishing town*, as one 1830s English tourist's guide referred to it. By the end of that century, however, because of the new-found passion for sea bathing and the king's presence in the town, a serious building boom began and land prices jumped by 500% as the wealthy competed with one another to build beautiful homes along the sea front and beyond. This popularity meant that Melcombe Regis' population also boomed, with an 83% increase between 1801 and 1821. Weymouth and Melcombe Regis were now tourist meccas.

By 1748, a pair of enterprising locals had applied for permission to put two bathing machines on Melcombe Regis' beach; eventually, even King George had one of his own, which of course was the grandest of them all. Those "machines" remained popular well into the 19th century and eventually there were dozens of them all along the seafront, some privately owned, some for rent to visitors. Along the South Parade there was also a hot salt bath business, with dressing rooms and other facilities that were popular during poor weather and with those who preferred to bathe inside rather than out.

WEYMOUTH BRIDGE .

Opposing views

The same tourist's guide describing Weymouth as *a mere fishing village* also described what Weymouth and Melcombe Regis (the two towns had been made one under royal decree in the 16th century, but maintained their own sense of identity through the end of the 19th century) looked like in 1831:

...the Duke of Gloucester, and afterwards of George III, and the royal family, with whom it was a favourite place of resort, laid the foundation of its present prosperity. The town is beautifully situated on the western shore of a fine open bay in the English Channel, and separated into two parts by the river Wey, which, expanding to a considerable breadth, in its progress to the bay, forms a small, but secure and commodious, harbour, on the south side of which is Weymouth, at the foot of a high hill near the mouth of the river; and, on

the north side, Melcombe Regis, on a peninsula, connected with the main land by a narrow isthmus, which separates the waters of the bay from those formed by the estuary of the river, called the Backwater. A long and handsome stone bridge of two arches, with a swivel in the centre, to admit small vessels into the upper part of the harbour has been erected by act of parliament.

That act was passed during George IV's reign.

Interestingly, about five years prior to that positive description, another was recorded and it was anything but glowing. When George III died in 1820, his Gloucester Lodge on the seafront was sold. In the mid-twenties, it was let out to a woman often referred to in her day as a "notorious socialite" and her husband, army officer and Member of Parliament Lord George Russell. His "notorious" wife was Elizabeth Anne Rawdon, and the couple lived locally for some years while Lord Russell was stationed at Dorchester Barracks. Lady Russell dubbed Weymouth and surrounds:

An aguish, nasty, noisy place...a horrid place I must own – the climate exceedingly disagreeable even to me who like warmth and the sea, but the air is enervating, a perpetual sirocco – sea fogs as hot as the steam of a tea kettle, and then a monotony quite deadening. One walk, one drive, one view, all the houses looking one way, and instead of a marine smell, one of pitch, tar, tallow, sea coal smoke and so forth.

This description may be harsh, but it is certainly useful when trying to get a sense of the hustle and bustle of the community in that era of its history.

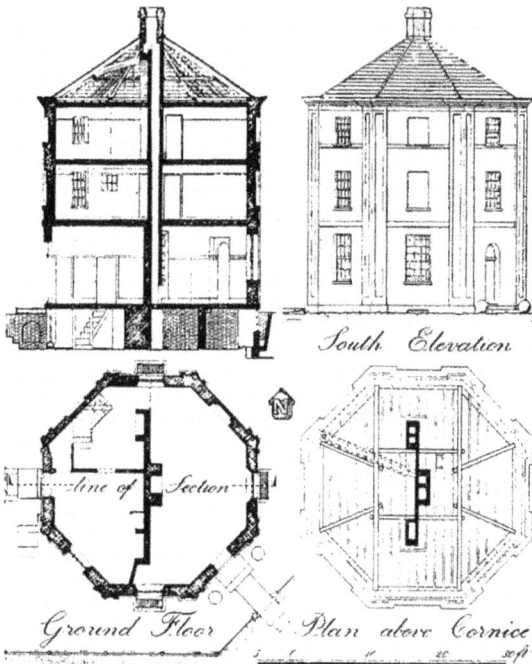

South Elevation

line of Section

Ground Floor

Plan above Cornice

NOTTINGTON SPA WEYMOUTH

Other water treatments

Although sea bathing remained popular throughout the 19th century, by the 1820s, it was rivalled by spa treatments. The Weymouth area had two popular spas, Nottington and Radipole. They were built over natural sulphurous springs which had been popular with locals long before the craze made them attractive to entrepreneurs. The spas were at their peak between the 1830s and the 1870s.

Nottington's rectangular spa house, built in 1830 and still standing, had two bath rooms, a dressing room, two sitting rooms, six chambers and a pump. People who could afford the treatments truly believed there were health benefits from the salty water, described in an advertisement about the sale of the Nottington spa in The Times newspaper in the 1850s:

A *highly valuable Freehold estate, comprising a substantial and well-built Spa house, with its valuable and medicinal flowing hydrogen spring* and *The medical testimony in favour of this extraordinary spring exceeds belief in cases of gout, jaundice and other complaints."*

In order to continue to attract visitors and investment to the town, by the end of the 18th century Weymouth's streets were paved, street lamps were installed and kept lit by the town's lamplighter, and roads and walk ways were kept clear of animal waste and debris. Locals could no longer graze their stock on Melcombe Common or other open grounds in and around town, which was intended to assure the spacious green areas were attractive to the local elite and wealthy visitors, although this did not please locals who had exercised their public grazing rights there for centuries.

The need for clean water also increased because of the growing population, which led Parliament in 1797 to vote to give permission to build a municipal water system in order to supply the town. Clean water was piped from Preston's "Boiling Rock," below Chalbury Hill, a spring that had been the water supply for the Neolithic people living there thousands of years prior. The pipeline ran through Lodmoor and in to Melcombe Regis. There was also an impressive new turnpike built which followed the old Roman road through Preston and along the seafront and there was even a law passed in the 1790s making it illegal for any of the new buildings going up around the town to have thatched roofs. Fire sweeping through Weymouth and its neighbours had been a serious threat for centuries; in the 1600s, Charles II had contributed thousands of pounds to the town to help it rebuild after an especially devastating fire.

There were also new rows and terraces being built, some of them with names inspired by the king's presence in the town, like Charlotte Row, Augusta Place, Gloucester Row and Royal Terrace. Then there were the new, modern buildings like the Clarence, Devonshire and Pulteney. Member of Parliament Sir William Pulteney built a row of homes known as the Pulteney Buildings on the Esplanade in 1805; he and his wife both inherited fortunes, his from a family member in Bath, where the couple lived. The MP, who many referred to as the wealthiest man in Great Britain, considered both Weymouth and Bath important enough to spend a lot of the couple's money building impressive structures in their centres. When Sir William died, his estate went to his daughter, Henrietta Pulteney, First Countess of Bath, who was married to General Sir James Murray Pulteney (the general added his wife's surname to his own because of his father-in-law's fame and fortune), MP for Weymouth and Melcombe Regis from 1790 to 1811.

There was also the impressive home of the king himself; George III purchased his brother's home, Gloucester Lodge, and enlarged it to become the Royal Lodge, with its beautiful views of the bay. Further up the Esplanade there were assembly and card rooms, like *John Harvey's Library and Card Assembly*, where wealthy guests could have tea, play cards, read newspapers and books and even dance, but only in a very staid manor. An elegant public library and a number of privately owned libraries that "let out" books for a small charge were also very popular as was the Royal Hotel with its large stables and meeting rooms which attracted wealthy guests.

The town's theatre was well equipped and hosted many plays for up to 300 guests at a time; it was open four nights a week during "the season," which ran from Christmas to mid-summer. And by the second decade of the 19th century, one of the most popular local entertainments was the Weymouth racecourse, located near Lodmoor.

Chapeau d'Espagne

The first horse races were held at the Weymouth racecourse in 1821. The local patrons of the course were Lord George Bentinck and a Mr. Fulwar Craven. Bentinck was a Conservative MP, closely allied with Prime Minister Benjamin Disraeli. He was also the grandson of William Bentinck, 3rd Duke of Portland, advisor to King William III, twice prime minister, Chancellor of Oxford and the great, great, great grandfather of Queen Elizabeth II. George Bentinck was also an avid racehorse owner and serious gambler; in the 1845 season alone, he won over £100,000, the equivalent of about £4.5 million today.

Fulwar Craven came from a long line of Lords and landowners who were also serious racehorse owners and breeders. These men knew one another well and frequently placed their horses in the same races; those thoroughbreds had wonderful names like Chapeau d'Espagne, Crucifix and Deception, and they competed at racecourses around the country, to include Weymouth's.

The principal races at this racecourse were the Weymouth Gold Cup which ran over 2.5 miles; the Lodmoor Stakes at 1.5 miles; the Mount Harrier Stakes, also 1.5 miles; the Weymouth Silver Cup at 2 miles and 1 furlong; the Weymouth Queen's Plate; the Weymouth Member's Plate; and the Tradesmen's Selling Plate at just over 2.5 miles. The Tradesmen's race was unique in that the horse that won the race was auctioned to the highest bidder after the heat.

The burning cliffs of Holworth

Mary Anning, the teenager from Lyme Regis who in the late 18th century became the world's first palaeontologist, brought the Dorset coast into the national and international spotlight with her finds of "ancient creatures": dinosaurs. Despite the fact that Anning's knowledge of dinosaurs was incredible and whose work was respected by early palaeontologists and geologists of the 19th century, because she was a woman, she was not given the respect that a man with the same abilities would have been and she complained that *The world has used me so unkindly…* when speaking of her life's experiences, but it was her work that opened up a whole new field in the sciences.

Today, it is still Lyme Regis that is best known for its Blue Lias rock formations, the type of limestone that does such a good job of preserving fossils, however, in the early 19th century, a smaller but significant find of Blue Lias was also found in Melcombe Regis. When sliced open, it revealed ammonites and spar, a rock with crystal-like formations inside. This discovery added Melcombe to the list of favourite destinations for naturalists, but it was a much bigger natural phenomenon that brought even more visitors to the area. It was dubbed the "Burning Cliffs of Holworth."

In about 1815 near the boundary of South Holworth Farm, not far from Osmington, the origins of the "burning cliffs" began with the movement of earth and stone near Holworth Cliff. Over another twelve years, the earth shifted and a mass of strange stone sank toward the sea, taking the cottage of a local fisherman with it. As the movement increased, it revealed something stone-like that was at the time compared to Kimmeridge coal which was *used as an article of fuel by the neighbouring poor,* but part of the stone was also composed of the same Blue Lias found in Lyme Regis and Melcombe Regis.

Beginning in 1827, the fire that had actually been burning "under" the rock for some time began to cause smoke to come to the surface through fissures, and then, flames sometimes reaching an estimated height of seventy feet appeared. Witnesses at the time described the fire as creating an "inexpressible grandeur." A national magazine published an extensive article about the phenomenon and described the stone as *of a strong bituminous and sulphureous nature; it burns free, and produces a very brilliant light, but emits at first, and until the gaseous particles are all evaporated, a very offensive smell.*

Another national magazine described it as *There are now upwards of twenty apertures extending in a line from east to west between ninety and a hundred feet. About the centre of this line of exhalations there is one aperture, assuming the appearance of a volcanic crater, exhibiting within very vivid burning lime-stone, the upper portion lined with shining black bituminous shale, and around the exterior of the orifice a large quantity of brilliant crystallized sulphur.* And nineteenth and early twentieth century travel guides described it as *like a miniature Vesuvius, converting Weymouth Bay by day and night into a closer resemblance to the Bay of Naples than ever before contemplated by travellers.*

The burning cliffs attracted lots of visitors to Weymouth and its surrounding communities and those who wanted to see them up close travelled in traps and small wagons toward Osmington and had to walk toward the cliffs, often accompanied by enterprising locals who offered their services as tour guides. There were so many visitors, some self-proclaimed naturalists who wanted to discover the secrets of the burning cliffs and others who wanted to carry off chunks of the material as mementos of their trip, that they trampled the garden of the former cottage of the fisherman, one that had been well known for its fine fruit trees and vegetables; the vegetation was so fine because of the structure of the soil near the burning cliffs. After a few years of these visitors tramping around, though, *now the numerous trespassing visitors have nearly obliterated every vestige of so remarkable an occurrence.*

Europe Is At Our Feet...

The Napoleonic Wars, which began with the French Revolution, were actually a series of conflicts at the end of which Napoleon Bonaparte, a Corsican military officer, proclaimed himself emperor of France. Ruling France was not enough for him, however, and he set his sights on conquering all of Europe and beyond. As he made his plans, Napoleon was especially concerned with the English, who he declared the French *must destroy the English monarchy, or expect itself to be destroyed by those intriguing and enterprising islanders...Let us concentrate all our efforts on the navy and annihilate England. That done, Europe is at our feet.* That was in 1797.

Although the conflict with the French had its roots in the French Revolution, the war against Napoleon was not formally declared by the British until 1803 and finally ended in 1815, when the French were defeated once and for all by the English.

As with other eras in English history, Dorset played an important part in helping to fight and win the Napoleonic Wars, especially Weymouth and its neighbours. As in other centuries, Dorset farmers grew the hemp and flax used by local weavers to produce the heavy cloth for naval ships' sails. Local sail makers produced hundreds of sails, while the cordage makers were kept busy making rigging ropes, also for naval ships, also made from locally grown hemp. Vital food was produced for the King's fleets; beer, bread, and other food provisions were prepared in vast quantities and local merchants sold guns, shot, gunpowder, muskets, swords, and bandoliers to the military. Even the tailors were kept busy making uniforms out of locally grown hemp and wool and cobblers made sturdy boots out of locally produced leather. And then there were the "holystones."

Possibly the most unique of all the military provisions produced locally, Portland quarrymen made soft limestone scrubbers, known as holystones, which were used to clean the decks of naval vessels from the late 18th to the early 20th century; the name comes from the fact that in order for seamen to use them, they had to kneel, as if in prayer, when they were "holystoning the deck."

Radipool

As the political upheavals of the Napoleonic era rocked Europe, the Germanic states were some of the hardest hit. Hanoverian kings had ruled Great Britain since 1714 with George III's reign lasting from 1760 to 1820, making him king throughout this time period. In 1803, his father's and grandfather's native Hanover — though the first of the Hanoverian rulers born in London rather than Germany, George III also continued to act as the Elector of Hanover - was invaded by Napoleon. That state's army had to disband, with the exception of the men and officers who became the King's German Regiment, George's special battalion; they were also known as the Hussars.

The German Regiment consisted of a number of units, also called regiments, and included cavalry and "heavy-dragoons," along with other specialised groups. When they were in Dorset, they were based in Weymouth, most of them living in the fields of Radipole and along the Bincombe Downs, with thousands of soldiers encamped at any given time of the year. Their presence was a constant throughout the Napoleonic Wars.

One German officer wrote about his experiences when he stayed in Weymouth, which provides a clear and entertaining picture of local life at the time. In about 1803, the officer, who preferred to remain anonymous, described the Radipole quarters:

About the middle of January our regiment changed quarters with the heavy-dragoon regiment of our legion, which, until, had been stationed at Radipool. As the barracks at this place were larger than those of Dorchester, I took up my abode therein. They belonged, however, to the temporary class before alluded to, and stood hardly more than two gun-shots' distance from the sea-shore. They were of brick, and only one story high. Although it was now the middle of winter, men were employed in enlarging these barracks still more. The rooms were six feet long and proportionably broad, and were abundantly supplied with every comfort, excepting beds, by the barrack-master.

There were also extensive military buildings going up in and around Dorchester and Weymouth from the late 18th into the first years of the 19th century. This was done at the behest of Prime Minister William Pitt, who believed impressive military buildings enhanced national safety. There were even official "barracks' architects" in the war department. They designed Weymouth's facilities near the harbour, which burned down only a year after they were built in 1798. Those were re-built in 1801 near the Nothe and were dubbed the Red Barracks because they were made from red brick. The buildings housed at least a dozen officers, almost 400 non-commissioned officers and soldiers, as well as a hospital and a large parade ground and stables, an impressive sight at the time.

Bincombe's Romeo and Juliet

Phyllis used to say that his English, though not good, was quite intelligible to her, so that their acquaintance was never hindered by difficulties of speech.

Dorset Author Thomas Hardye

Only a few miles from the centre of Weymouth sits a tiny little village called Bincombe, with its Saxon-Medieval church and Bincombe Bumps, a series of Neolithic burial mounds above the village. In 1801, a doctor's daughter, Phyllis Grove, was living in a small, dilapidated house at the bottom of the village's hill. She was an only child whose mother had died when the girl was very young. Doctor Grove was a morose, depressed man whose practice had long since failed and Phyllis lived a solitary life, keeping house for her father and attending church every Sunday.

Probably on her father's insistence, Phyllis had become engaged to a local merchant, Humphrey Gould. He was a cold man who travelled a great in his work and who did not pay very much attention to the quiet girl. The only break in Phyllis' solitude was when the King's German Legion arrived with thousands of soldiers camping along the Bincombe Downs under their billowing white tents. During one of those visits, she was strolling along the bottom of the downs when Phyllis met Matthaus, a young German corporal with the York Hussars.

Over time, the two continued to meet clandestinely and they fell in love. Matthous asked her to run away with him back to his native Germany and Phyllis agreed. The plan included Matthous' friend Christoph, another young German corporal, who was going to "borrow" a boat from Weymouth harbour to help the couple escape. Phyllis packed a few of her belongings and waited for her lover at the appointed time, on the road where Bincombe met the main Dorchester to Weymouth highway.

As she waited, the long distance coach pulled up and out stepped Phyllis' fiancé. The girl's conscience pricked her and when Matthous arrived shortly afterward, she told him she could not run away with him. Heartbroken, he felt he could not leave his friend at the harbour and the two Germans paddled off toward France, where they planned to go on to Germany.

Also heartbroken, Phyllis met with Humphrey Gould after she had broken the news to Matthous; Gould informed her that he had married on the sly and even asked her to break the news to her father, afraid of the doctor's reaction. The girl was devastated and grieved over her decision not to leave for Germany with her true love.

Not a week later, Phyllis was sitting on the village wall, something she did every day as she daydreamed about Matthous, when along came a band playing the Trauermarsch, the "march of the dead." The band was accompanied by a procession of soldiers, two coffins and two accompanying priests. These were followed by two other soldiers, both blindfolded. Not far from the church, the group stopped beside the coffins and the two soldiers knelt next to the coffins and appeared to be praying. The commanding officer gave a signal and the soldiers, who had lined up, guns ready, shot the two men.

Realising who the soldiers were, Phyllis was so shocked she fell off of the wall. It turned out Matthous and Christoph had mistakenly landed at Guernsey and were caught and brought back to face court martial in Weymouth. They were found guilty of desertion and theft. Phyllis was so distraught at her lover's death, her father thought she was losing her sanity.

Many years later, when she was 75, she shared her story with Dorset writer Thomas Hardy, who was only 15-years-old at the time. Phyllis made him promise he would not tell anyone about it until after she died. He kept his word and wrote about the ill-fated couple many years later; he called their story **The Melancholy Hussar of the German Legion**.

The Dorchester and Sherborne Journal

On the 30 June, 1801, the local paper recorded the German's deaths this way: '...two of the York Hussars were shot on Bincombe Down, near Weymouth, pursuant to the sentence of a Court Martial, for desertion and cutting a boat out of the harbour with intent to go into France, but by mistake they landed at Guernsey and were secured. All the regiments both in camp and barracks were drawn up, viz. the Greys, the Rifle Corps, and the Stafford, Berks, and North Devon Militia. They came on the ground in a mourning coach, attended by two Priests; after marching along the front of the line they returned to the centre where they spent about 20 minutes in prayer, and were then shot at by a guard of 24 men. They dropped instantly and expired without a groan. They appeared sensible of their awful situation and very penitent. The men then wheeled in sections, and marched by the bodies in slow time.'

The parish register of Bincombe recorded the men's fate this way:

Mats. Tina (Corpl.) in his Majesty's Regmt. of York Hussars and Shot for desertion, was buried June 30th 1801 aged 22 years. Born in the town of Sarbruck, Germany. Christopher Bless belonging to his Majesty's Regmt. of York Hussars who was shot for desertion was buried June 30th 1801 aged 22 years, born at Lothaargen, Alsatia.

Their coffins were buried in the cemetery of Bincombe's church, where there is a very worn headstone still marking their graves, probably placed there by Phyllis.

The Arrival of the Aigle

His Majesty thinks it necessary to acquaint the House of Commons, that, as very considerable military

preparations are carrying on in the ports of France and Holland, he was judged it expedient to adopt

additional measures of precaution for the security of his dominions.

A message from George III to Parliament, March 1803

During the French Revolution, Prime Minister William Pitt introduced the Quota Acts. These were intended to supply the navy with sufficient manpower during a time when there were heightened fears that the French might cross the English Channel with the intention of invading. Under the acts, each county was required to provide their quota of men based on the population of the county. As a way of encouraging volunteers to come forward, most counties offered some kind of financial incentive but this was not sufficient motivation and the authorities resorted to recruiting in the prisons where able-bodied men were given the choice of joining the navy or serving out their sentences. Even this failed to produce enough potential sailors, so the navy used impressment, something that had been practiced for centuries, to fill its ranks. The first big push to impress local men, however, was not the success that the naval officers in charge had hoped it would be.

In early spring of 1803, Portsmouth Captain George Wolfe and his brand new frigate the Aigle were ordered to Dorset to impress seamen and to try to find volunteers who might join without force; he landed at Portland Roads and though his orders stated that he was to impress men from Portland and the local area, he went to Weymouth to seek the support of Weymouth's mayor and local merchant Samuel Weston. Mayor Weston informed the captain that when the Aigle had been spotted entering the port, the seamen working at Weymouth harbour rushed one of their own to Portland to ask the quarrymen to join the port labourers in resisting any attempts to impress them; impressment was nothing new and the arrival of an unfamiliar naval ship was always suspect.

The impressment gang from the Aigle rowed to Weymouth Quay, where they met with violent resistance from the seamen and quarrymen. The gang scrambled back to their boats in quick retreat. Not wanting to appear weak by giving in to the resistance, Captain Wolfe sailed his frigate to the top of the harbour of Portland where his gang disembarked but were again met by a group of seamen, some firing muskets at Wolfe and his men. This led to a fierce fight during which Wolfe took two prisoners, one armed with a poker, the other with a reaping hook. The locals dispersed to find reinforcements and another 300 men arrived armed with muskets, pistols and cutlasses that had been "liberated" from ships run aground some years before. It is not difficult to understand the Portlanders' response to Wolfe's attempts. Charles II

Quarrymen and Fishermen

Sydney Heath, an illustrator and writer, wrote at least three books about various aspects of life in Dorset and in one of those, The South Devon and Dorset Coast, written in 1910, he briefly described life for some local villagers at the turn of the 20th century.

At the back of the Chesil, and on the landward side of the east and west fleets, lie Chickerell, Fleet, and Langton Herring, which, although situated in valleys some mile or so from the coast, are typical fishing villages, the inhabitants of which depend on fishing and farming for a livelihood, in the same way that the natives of Portland combine seafaring with stone-quarrying. When the 'huer', who is always on the lookout, gives notice that a shoal of mackerel are approaching the shore, the natives, leaving plough, stone-quarry, or hay-cart, hurry down to the shallow fleets, which they cross in flat-bottomed punts, and pay out the seine nets from the cumbersome boats that always lie in readiness. To watch a good haul of mackerel taken on the Chesil is a sight worth going many miles to see. Men, women, and children leave their village homes in charge of the aged 'granfers' and 'granmers' and help to sort and pack the writhing masses of fish. Boxes and packing-cases of all descriptions are pressed into service, while frequently, so heavy is the catch, that when even the hen-coops have been converted into improvised packing-cases, thousands of fish lie rotting on the beach. By the light of oil flares, the packing and carting of fish sometimes continues far into the summer night.

had made it illegal to impress Portland seamen who served on the ships carrying Portland stone to London during the King's reconstruction of the city after the Great Fire of 1666 and in 1798, Weymouth seamen were also made exempt from impressment. Either the Royal Navy leaders were unaware of this or simply did not care.

Seventeen of Wolfe's men were severely wounded, some of whom never returned to military service because of their injuries. Wolfe, who was also badly hurt, probably would have died if it had not been for one of his seamen coming to his aid. Despite his injuries, he made the decision to call upon the marines who were also travelling on the Aigle to shoot into the crowd. Four local men were killed, the rest ran away from the mess, with only four caught as they tried to flee. But the story does not end there.

Captain Wolfe and his party made their way back to the frigate and he sent quick word to the admiralty to let them know what kind of resistance he and his men had encountered. Then he sailed back to Weymouth harbour where he was met by yet another mob who grabbed him and one midshipman off the ship and took them to the mayor, who was pressured to sign the committal of the two men. The mayor then sent the naval men to Dorchester gaol, charged with the murder of the locals killed by the Aigle's marines. The mob was still not satisfied, though; immediately after the mayor's actions, the coroner held an inquest where he agreed to a verdict of murder against the captain and three of his men. The intention was to keep them imprisoned in the Dorchester gaol until the summer assizes, but the war with Napoleon was imminent and the story was getting a lot of attention from outside of the area; the notoriety seemed to help settle the angry mob down. Wolfe and his men were granted bail and permitted to re-join their ship, where the captain had a bit of luck when cruising the Channel: he captured four fully loaded French West Indiamen, making him and his men quite rich.

When the murder trial took place, all of the charges were dropped against the sailors, as the jury declared the military men had acted in self-defence. That verdict came in spite of a statement against the captain by the coroner himself. During the battle between the military from the Aigle and the Portland mob, the sister of Robert Way, one of the two Portland men Wolfe had impressed, was badly injured. The coroner told the jury that she had told him, on her deathbed, that it was Wolfe who had shot her. The jury rejected this evidence and the captain sent the Way family two guineas and released the brother from his impressment.

In spite of his actions, when the mayor promised to provide the captain *with a sufficient number of constables to assist him and preserve order* so that Wolfe could get back to the business of "recruiting," the mayor once again proved he was still an instrument of the mob, not the king. He provided only two constables to help and Wolfe found, as he tried to land at Weymouth harbour, those constables were actually urging the mob on, not dispersing it.

Captain Wolfe had had enough of the locals and decided to leave the men of Weymouth and Portland to themselves; the Napoleonic Wars began in earnest just a few weeks later, declared on the 18th of May 1803. The Portlanders who died in their battle against impressment were buried in the graveyard of St. George's Church on Portland, where their headstones record them as the "Portland Martyrs."

The tone of the people at large…

An early 20th century clergyman wrote about the local people's response to Captain Wolfe's attempts to impress local men and his explanation provides interesting detail about local life:

These instances illustrate the tone of the people at large. The Weymouth of that date was a small port containing a number of locally owned and built small coasting craft, doing a lucrative trade which plied between Weymouth and Sunderland. In war-time they boldly kept the sea, fought their way back and forth, and made excellent freights. The same family often built, owned, manned, and made a comfortable living out of the same craft. They did not want their seamen taken off, and their trade hindered, by the Navy. The more adventurous built and fitted out vessels for privateering. These hated the idea of impressment more bitterly still. The fishing population also infinitely preferred the often excellent profits of smuggling, and the then well-paying fishing, to being forced on board a man-o'-war to endure the hardships and injustices such as caused the mutinies of 1797 <when angry sailors rioted against the bad treatment they received from their officers>. Patriotism, the danger and need of their country, then entering on the life – and – death struggle with Napoleon, did not appeal to them. Such considerations passed over their heads in their remote corner of Dorset and then out-of-the-way part of the kingdom, removed as they were from wider national interests and clinging tenaciously to their lawless pursuits. It is not a pleasant glimpse we obtain.

The Rev. W. Owen Cockcraft

1804

I cannot deny I am rather hurt there is any objection made to forming so large an army of reserves in Dorset

where, or in Cornwall, I think an attack more likely than in Essex, Kent or Sussex.

King George III to his son, the Commander in Chief, about his plans to guard against
French invasion in June, 1804

Local seamen and quarrymen may not have been, for obvious reasons, keen on the idea of being impressed in to the Royal Navy, but the many soldiers and sailors who were familiar sites to local residents at the end of the 18th into the 19th centuries were joined during the Napoleonic Wars by local men who volunteered to serve. This was in part because the government by that time was convinced that invasion by French troops was inevitable and the average Englishman took the threat to his safety more and more seriously. It is not surprising given that in 1804, Napoleon had achieved his aim of conquering all of Europe. Interestingly, George III was sure that Dorset was one of the emperor's primary British targets, as Napoleon made his plans to *concentrate all our efforts on the navy and annihilate England.*

In order to encourage volunteering, the British government began a campaign to raise thousands of recruits in the south. Part of the recruitment process was to post notices on all church doors, promising a shilling a day:

You will find your best recompense in having done your duty to King and Country by driving back or destroying your old implacable enemy envious of your Freedom and Happiness, and therefore seeking to destroy them and in having protected your Wives and Children from Death or worse than death, which would follow the success of your Inveterate Foes.

> **Happy Birthday to the Prince**
>
> In addition to their regular training, the Sea Fencibles also had ceremonial duties. They were featured in the newspapers of the day when the royal family arrived in Portland Roads, from Weymouth, on board the HMS Cambrian on 12 August 1800. They and the local militias gathered at Portland Castle, which had been renovated as part of the war effort, where local militias joined the festivities by firing the appropriate salutes and a further salute to celebrate the birthday of George, the Prince of Wales.

There had been local militias serving Dorset for centuries, and by 1804, locals were stepping up to volunteer to protect their community. Portlanders heeded the call and signed up for their own "Legion of Volunteers," with over 100 men serving; their purpose was not to join the navy or to go to Europe to fight, but to defend the island from the expected French invasion. Some of them were members of the Sea Fencibles. This was a volunteer force created through an act of Parliament in 1798, also a result of the fear of French attack. Many members of this special legion were recruited amongst local seamen and fishermen, who were exempt from impressment. It was the job of those men to create a ring around Britain to assure the entire coast was secure.

Lives are lent for laws and King

When that they may need 'em;

Let us then in chorus sing,

Give us death or freedom.

To the fields of Mars advance,

Join in the bold alliance!

Tell the blood stain'd Sons of France

We bid them all defiance. The local volunteers own "anti-Napoleon" song

The captain of Portland's volunteer legion was the island's governor John Penn. Perhaps better known for the magnificent home he built on the island, Pennsylvania Castle, than for his local leadership, Penn was a favourite of King George III, who awarded him the governorship. Penn was the grandson of the founder of the American colony of Pennsylvania, hence the commemorative name of his Portland stone "castle." It was natural for him to accept the post of both governor and captain given part of King George's reasoning for awarding Penn, whose mother was one of Queen Charlotte's ladies in waiting, such a large area of land. It helped assure the king had a trusted ally watching the Channel from such an important vantage point, ready and willing to report any espionage activity by the French fleet.

In spite of being the great grandson of the famous Admiral of the Blue, William Penn, father of William Penn, the founder of the state of Pennsylvania, John Penn was a very shy man, far more interested in studying the classics and writing than seeking fame and fortune. He was very involved in writing and directing plays, working with local actors to present his works in Weymouth or as he described in it in 1831 in the dedication of his book *The Battle of Eddington; or, British Liberty, Tragedy*, which he wrote at Pennsylvania Castle:

I have, during the late rejoicings at our success in political undertakings, furnished to the Theatre, an attempt to contribute to the amusement of the neighbouring watering-place of Weymouth, through the medium of a company of Actors, by a novel construction of a tragic Drama.

Penn wrote this to his friend Lord Ashley, Dorchester MP and son of the Lord of Shaftsbury.

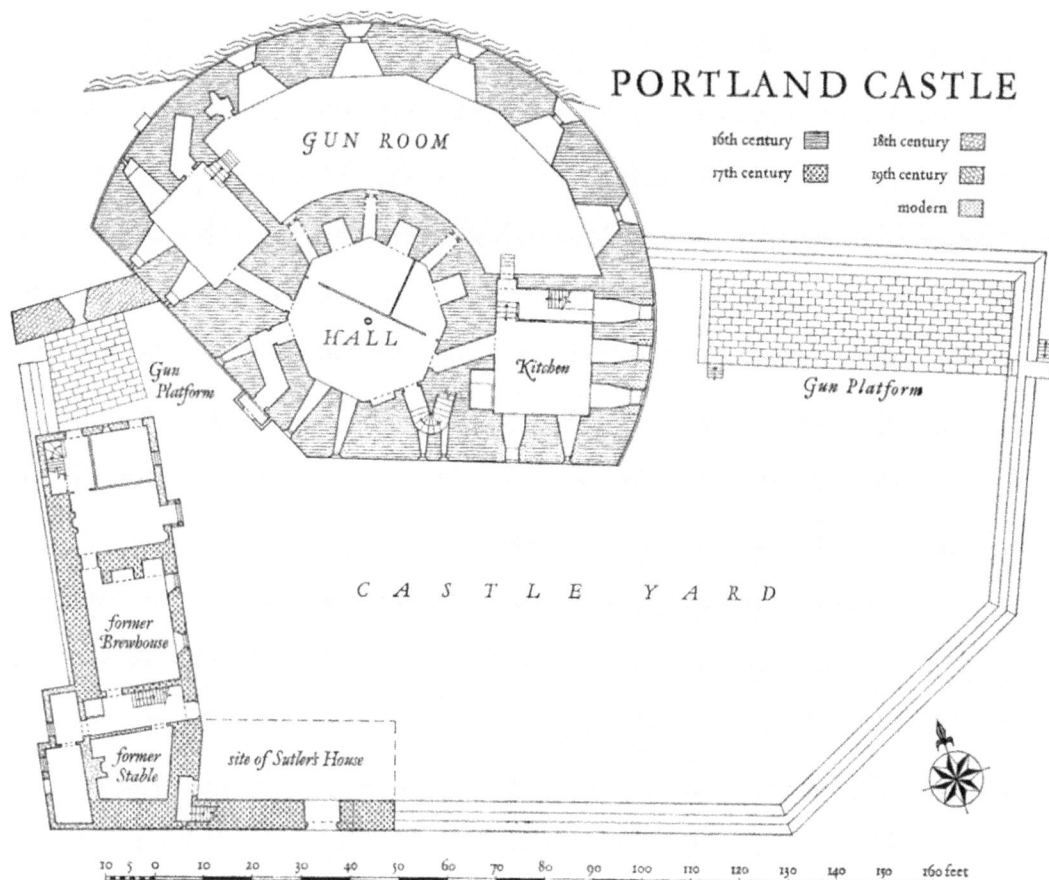

PORTLAND CASTLE

GUN ROOM

16th century ▦   18th century ▨
17th century ▩   19th century ▧
                  modern ▢

HALL

Gun Platform

Kitchen

Gun Platform

CASTLE YARD

former Brewhouse

former Stable

site of Sutler's House

10 5 0   10   20   30   40   50   60   70   80   90   100   110   120   130   140   150   160 feet

A Marine Residence

Portland Castle, built by Henry VIII next to a Saxon fortress, was intended to help protect Portland Harbour, to provide a temporary home for the goods taken from monasteries after the Dissolution, and as a prison. By 1816 (some sources have it at 1818), the French threat was considered over, making the castle's military roll redundant. It was decided to grant Portland Castle to the rector of Portland, Reverend John Manning, by H.R.H. Prince Edward, the fourth son of George III, as a 'marine residence'. Manning spent a lot of money renovating the castle and probably began the work on what became known as the Captain's House, a separate residence next to the castle which incorporated parts of former outbuildings, replacing the castle's brewery, stables, and the home of the sutler, a merchant who sold goods to the military. The reverend died in 1826 and by 1834, his son, Captain Charles Manning, was granted the castle, also as a residence.

After Queen Victoria took the throne, the castle was granted officially to Captain Manning who also became the Lieutenant of the Island and Resident Magistrate. Prince Albert visited the castle in 1843 and remarked on how tasteful the decoration was; a local guide book from the time described the entrance hall as ...*tastefully fitted up as the armoury, and in which are many implements of warfare, both ancient and modern, kept in a state of neatness and order rarely equalled, and which was remarked by his Royal Highness Prince Albert.* When the captain died in 1869, the castle was returned to military duty as the home of the adjutant of Verne Citadel and later, it played a part in WWI and saw a Royal Navy station built near it, where anti-submarine patrols flew to and from, using seaplanes, a new invention from France.

Penn's lieutenants were Henry Lowman and Richard Lano and the Portland Legion was made up of eight non-commissioned officers, four drummers and 103 privates. By May 1804, the legion was on permanent duty *on a report of the enemy being about to land on the island.* Other groups serving in the local legions were volunteers from Upwey, Broadhayes, Radipole, Fleet, and Wyke Regis. Weymouth had the biggest contingent with almost 140 men, to include one-time mayor Major Samuel Weston, numerous lieutenants, and eleven non-commissioned officers. A number of the volunteers were not only ship owners, they were also privateers and must have been a great asset given how much they knew about the local coastline.

Men in each parish were called up to serve in the militia and they did this by drawing lots. If a man's lot was drawn and he did not want to serve, he could find a substitute to go in his place. The replacement was usually paid £7, about £240 today, making this something only a man of means could afford to do.

Local war heroes...

Although the stories of most of the men who served in the local regiments have been lost to history, Dorset did have its own heroes. Weymouth surgeon John Bullen became the Surgeon General of North America to the Royal Navy in 1779. His son Charles Bullen, who was born in Newcastle-upon-Tyne but who spent most of his childhood in Weymouth, accompanied his father to New York, eventually joining the navy and serving throughout the Napoleonic Wars. He was the captain of HMS Britannia at the battle of Trafalgar in 1805, one of the most important naval battles fought during the wars, and eventually retired back to Weymouth.

Another Dorset man, Captain Henry Digby, was captain of the HMS Africa, also at the Battle of Trafalgar. His uncle was Admiral Robert Digby of the tiny village of Minterne Magna, not far from Weymouth. The Digbys had purchased the ancient estate from the Churchill family and Henry Digby inherited it from his uncle; Henry Digby died there in 1842.

Our captain was Hardy, the pride of us all,

I'll ask for none better when danger shall call.

He was hardy by nature and Hardy by name.

And soon by his conduct to honour he came.

Thomas Masterman Hardy was born in 1769 in the parish of Long Bredy. He joined the Navy in 1781 where he served under Admiral Horatio Nelson for several years before joining HMS Victory in 1803. He played a major role as Nelson's Flag-Captain at the Battle of Trafalgar, during which Nelson lost his life. Hardy was made a baronet in 1806, became Commodore in the Portuguese Navy in 1811, and in 1815 he was made a Knight Commander of the Order of the Bath. He returned to England in 1824, became a Rear Admiral a year later and in 1834, Hardy was appointed Governor of Greenwich Hospital and then promoted to Vice-Admiral in 1837. During his long career, Hardy inherited a Tudor home, Goose Hill, built by an ancestor five miles from Weymouth in the village of Portesham and had it remodelled in the Georgian style; it still stands today. Though he returned to his home on and off, he died in Greenwich in 1839.

The Beacons

As with other centuries, along the Dorset coast and around the rest of the country's coastline, during the 19th century there were beacons set up in order to assure those who were watching out for the arrival of French ships could alert the residents. These sat on the highest promontories and were fuelled by rushes. The only time on record that they were lit during the Napoleonic wars was in Bridport and that occasion illustrates just how nervous the British, especially those living near the English Channel, were about Napoleon's threats.

In April, 1799, a Dorset newspaper printed a story about the commanding officer of Bridport; late one night he received a message from a neighbouring signal house, small facilities with their own beacons, telling him that the French were landing *in the west*. Unfortunately, it also said that the officer did not know how many French had landed or their exact location, promising that information by the next morning. The Bridport volunteers called their drummers in to *beat to arms* and they lit up their beacons. The three companies of Bridport volunteers assembled quickly, ready to march wherever they were ordered, as were a small contingent of Somerset Provisional cavalrymen and Dorset Yeomantry.

A local publication noted that they *assembled from all quarters with the greatest expedition; Captain Prater and the Sea Fencibles were at the batteries the whole of a very severe night; the neighbouring companies were also in a state of preparation. The loyalty of each corps cannot be too much applauded, and the anxiety to meet the enemy could not be exceeded by any regular troops. About seven in the morning intelligence was received that a mistake had been made at the signal house.* Some of the men believed this was an intentional exercise, but the majority view was someone had made a mistake, reporting a merchant ship unloading along the coast, not invading French.

Panic-stricken bumpkins…

The king's safety when he was visiting Weymouth was paramount as the war progressed, so much so that there was a grand plan to whisk him away to London should Dorset be invaded; his coach was always on standby whenever he was staying at his seafront home. That was in spite of the fact that there were always at least 500 King's German Legion soldiers posted locally along with hundreds of local volunteer units. In May 1804, the king's worries seemed to be realised. He and his family were visiting when news reached Weymouth that the French fleet had been spotted landing on Portland. There was a heavy fog that morning and the signal stations along the coast at Abbotsbury, Golden Cap and at the Verne had no visibility, which meant the news came from local coastguards struggling to see through the fog.

Word was sent to all of the volunteer units who grabbed whatever meagre weapons they had and headed toward Portland. Meanwhile, the women of Weymouth and Portland packed what they could carry and headed out of town toward Bere Regis; the local priests were in their churches praying for the safety of the community. Word soon spread as far as Lulworth and Dorchester, where residents were also in a panic. Fortunately, it was soon realised there was no French fleet, what the coastguard had spotted was a group of fishing boats. The incident was noted in Parliament when an MP referred to the local residents as *panic-stricken bumpkins.*

Imposs*ible* !

False alarms or no, there is no doubt that the entire West Coast lived in dread of invasion and there was, from 1804 well into the 20th century, an enduring Dorset legend about Napoleon. The wife of a local farmer and part-time smuggler had learned to speak French as a child when she travelled with her father who had had a china import business. All her life, until she died in 1888 at the age of 104, the farmer's wife told the story of how early one morning she was standing not far from Lulworth Cove where she saw a ship anchored close to shore. There was a man on the beach, reading a map; she was convinced he was Napoleon when she heard him say in French *Impossible!* as he surveyed the cove in

---

The Book of Invasion

During this troubled era, a local resident recorded a plan of invasion for the local people. It included a kind of inventory listing the numbers of wagons and horses available in various villages that should be used to move women and children away from danger if the coast was invaded. The "Book of Invasion" even listed the cattle and sheep that should be moved and mentioned the men who were responsible for gathering available weapons, which included saws, axes and pickaxes.

disgust. The locals assumed Napoleon had chosen that quiet part of the coast to land his invading ships, but when he arrived to see the spot for himself, he realized his intelligence was wrong and decided against the plan because it was "impossible."

Hardy's Trumpet Major

The preparations to counter French invasion figure in at least three of Dorset author Thomas Hardy's works, especially in his book **The Trumpet Major**. Hardy's grandfather was a member of the Puddletown Volunteers and an amateur soldier and the humorous book was based on his experiences. Those local men were immensely keen, but had little military experience and Hardy used **The Trumpet Major's** drill sergeant to illustrate that fact:

"Attention, men. Now I hope you will have a little patience," said the sergeant, standing in the centre of an arc, "and pay attention strict to the word of command, exactly as I gave it to you, and if I go wrong, I shall be much obliged if any friend who'll put me right again for I have only been in the army myself three weeks and we are all liable to make mistakes. Attention, poise firelocks."

"'Please, what must we do if we haven't got no firelocks?" said the lower end of the line in a hopeless voice. Now was there ever such a question."

"'Why, you must do nothing at all. Just think how you would poise them if you had 'em. You middle men that are armed with hurdle staves and cabbage stumps just to make believe, must of course use them as if they were the real thing. Now then, cock firelocks, present, fire (pretend to, I mean and at the same time throw your imagination into the field of battle)."

In honour of his grandfather, Thomas Hardy wrote **The Alarm**, a poem which mentions Maiden Castle, the Ridgeway between Weymouth and Dorchester and the Sea Fencibles:

The Alarm

Then on he panted

By grim Mai-Don, and slanted

Up the steep Ridge-way, hearkening between whiles;

Till nearing coast and harbour he beheld the shore-line planted

With Foot and Horse for miles.

Mistrusting not the omen,

He gained the beach, where Yeomen

Militia, Fencibles and Pikesmen bold,

With Regulars in thousands, were enmassed to meet the Foemen,

Whose fleet had not yet shoaled.

But Buonoparte still tarried:

His project had miscarried;

At the last hour, equipped for victory,

The fleet had paused; his subtle combinations had been parried

Homeward returning

Anon, no beacons burning,

No alarms, the Volunteers, in modest bliss,

Te Deum sang with wife and friends: "We praise Thee, Lord, discerning

That Thou hast helped in this!"

Prisoners of war...

During the Napoleonic Wars, there were 102,000 French soldiers and sailors shipped to England to live as prisoners of war for the duration of the on-going conflict. This had not happened in previous wars when military, especially officers, were usually exchanged between the warring factions on the field of battle. Most of the French prisoners were held in coastal towns, to include Weymouth, which was designated a "parole" community; room was made in the Red Barracks facilities to house the Frenchmen.

The prisoners were not held under lock and key, they were allowed daily parole and signed contracts that limited their movements and the time they were allowed to be away from the barracks: "gentlemen's agreements." Many worked for local farmers installing drainage, constructing buildings, and planting hedgerows and trees. This would have been welcomed, as there was a shortage of labour because of the long and demanding conflict. What was probably not as welcome was the reputation some of the men had for "dallying" with local women. And what many locals would have been aware of was that some of the Frenchmen, especially the officers, who were paroled in other parole communities, somehow ended up in Weymouth "unofficially," a step toward getting back to France by paying a willing local fisherman-come-smuggler to take them home.

...George Culliford, a notorious smuggler, was committed to Ilchester Gaol for conveying from Wincanton several of the prisoners there to the Dorsetshire coast, whence crossed to Cherbourg. The Salisbury Journal, 1811

Culliford was not the only West Country smuggler who discovered early on in the Napoleonic Wars that there was money to be made from smuggling Frenchmen back to their home country. Because they were free to roam and likely to have access to money, it is estimated that almost 1,000 French officers hired smugglers to take them home and at least 55 of those left from Weymouth harbour to Cherbourg. The going rate for this trip was up to £500 pounds, which is almost £17,000 in today's money. Besides enriching local smugglers, it is also an indication of just how cosy a relationship the local smugglers had with the French who helped them sail in and out of Cherbourg without interference, something the English authorities were becoming aware of as the wars continued on. Like centuries before, government officials passed laws and brought in law enforcement to stop, or at least to limit, smuggling along the Dorset coast, but it took years for those attempts to slow smugglers down.

After So Long a Period of War...

As the Napoleonic Wars wore on, smuggling not only continued, it thrived, evidenced by those Frenchmen who could afford the extortionate fees demanded of them in order to return to their home country. But it was not just human contraband that made some of the local smugglers quite wealthy; though the English Channel is often thought of as a watery blockade between France and the UK at that time, there was plenty of business being done between the two sides. This was helped by the fact that the Channel Islands were a natural point of exchange for many goods and had become a centre for this illegal trade by the turn of the 19th century. A ferry service from Weymouth to the islands had begun in 1794 and a number of Weymouth families moved there and probably helped further Weymouth smugglers' control over the illegal trade.

For many centuries, the English had had a thirst for French wine and brandy, as well as fine silks and other products made by the French. Locally, coopers did a good business in producing specially designed kegs that were small enough to be carried on the backs of the smugglers' local helpers or tied to the saddles of their horses. In 1805, when the government began a more serious clampdown on smuggling than had been tried before, it focussed on the Channel Islands. By 1809, this was buoyed by the creation of the Preventative Waterguard, the precursor to the modern coastguard. The guard had a fleet of ships commanded by naval officers who patrolled the waters most susceptible to smuggling, meaning there was a great deal of activity along the Dorset coast. They were supposed to work with the "preventative men," government agents whose job it was to find and arrest smugglers; although that arm of the government had been around for centuries, in one form or another, they were never terribly successful, hence the increase rather than the decrease in smuggling, even during the long years of war.

It then gets into the hands of women...

An 1804 report written by an agent of Weymouth's Customs House provides a fantastic account of smuggling activity along the local coastline and indicates why the government stepped up efforts to stop the illegal trade:

The articles generally smuggled from this part of the coast are chiefly brandy, rum and geneva, to which may be added a small quantity of wine, tobacco and salt, the whole from the islands of Guernsey and Alderney, which are imported in casks containing from four to six gallons each in vessels from ten to thirty tons burthen in the winter, and in the summer season in boats from three to eight or nine tons carrying three hundred and fifty casks, which are generally sunk on rafts till a convenient opportunity offers for taking them up, which they put into boats and distribute them along the coast at Portland and on the beach called Chiswell Beach as far west as Burton Hive, which is about sixteen miles in extent. It then gets into the hands of women and others, who disperse it in small quantities in the country for five or six miles round, and what is not got rid of in this manner is conveyed on horses forty or fifty miles up the country; but when from tempestuous weather the smugglers cannot sink their goods, they then work to the eastward of that island and sink and disperse it in like manner.

The places for landing the smuggled goods to the eastward of this place are Jordan Gate, Upton Mills, Ringstead Beach, Mupe, Arish Mill and Worbarrow Beach. The three latter are the most noted places. It frequently happens that large vessels carrying from four to six or seven hundred casks land their cargoes at these places, which vessels do not belong to or are known to any in this part of the coast. This they carry off in waggons, carts or on horse, escorted by large gangs of smugglers in defiance to the officers on this station, but goods so brought come not with the calculation we have formed which, from the best information we have been able to collect, and which concurs with our opinion, we suppose may amount to ten thousand casks annually, but none of which we apprehend reaches the metropolis...

For all the centuries various kings and their agents had tried to stop smuggling around the UK, this description differs little from 17th century reports, also written by Weymouth customs officials.

Conceal Their Privations

...after so long a period of war in every part of Europe, many of the most daring professional men, discharged
from their occupation and averse to the daily labour of agricultural or mechanical employment, will be the
ready instruments of those desperate persons who have a little capital, and are hardly enough to engage in
this traffic... The Lords Commissioners to the Treasury on smuggling, 1815

If it were possible to gauge the average sufferings of classes, the probability is that in Dorsetshire the figure
would be lower with the regular farmer's labourers -- 'workfolk' as they call themselves -- than with the
adjoining class, the unattached labourers, approximating to the free labourers of the middle ages, who are to
be found in the larger villages and small towns of the county -- many of them, no doubt, descendants of the
old copyholders who were ousted from their little plots when the system of leasing large farms grew general.
They are, what the regular labourer is not, out of sight of patronage; and to be out of sight is to be out of mind
when misfortune arises, and pride or sensitiveness leads them to conceal their privations.

From Thomas Hardy's The Dorsetshire Labourer

When Napoleon was finally defeated by the British at the Battle of Waterloo in 1815, the long, protracted series of wars were finally over. That meant somewhere between 220,000 and 400,000 soldiers and sailors were dumped back in to their home towns, many of which had had thriving economies because of the war; Weymouth and its neighbours are an excellent example of a place where agricultural labourers and small businesses had done very well out of the conflict. However, the combination of the loss of business because of the war ending and too many available workers had a negative impact on the local economy. This along with other long term problems like the steep rise in the price of basic staples such as wheat – the price of bread trebled in 1816, in part because of excessive rain and one of the coldest summers on record – was devastating to many. Added to these, there was the national movement toward enclosure of once traditionally public lands, all of which contributed to an increase in poverty and homelessness. It was a trying time for small farmers, skilled labourers and returning military. In 1794, Dorset weekly wages averaged 7 shillings; in 1804, that rose to 8 shillings; in 1814, to just under 14 shillings, but from 1817 on, it remained steady at 7 shillings a week for the next 25 years. The earlier spikes in wages were directly connected to the war economy and the dramatic drop after 1817 was due to the impact the end of the war had had on the local economy.

The pounder

Some of the jobs held by local villagers are no longer familiar today. Weymouth and many Dorset towns and villages paid town criers, an office created in the medieval era to help make citizens aware of royal decrees, as well as national and local news. Another was the *chimney peeper*, whose sole job was to 'peep' up chimneys and to let the authorities know whose was dirty; house fires in an area where thatched roofs were so common meant this was quite an important job. Then there was the *Hayward* who collected any stray cattle that had wandered off of common grazing land, a job that paid four pence per head. There was also the *pounder*. His job was to receive the stray cattle from the *Hayward* and to place them in the town or village pound, an enclosure designed specifically for that purpose. There were also the specialist merchants, the *sutlers,* who sold wares to the military and often lived in their own military-provided homes at places like Portland Castle. And the *roper*, who made rope!

The Enclosure Acts

They hang the man and flog the woman

That steals the goose from off the common

But lets the greater villain loose

That steals from the goose

17th century English enclosure protest poem

Originally, enclosures of land took place through informal agreement between individual landowners. In 1604, after the first official "public enclosure," the process became more complex and often required authorisation by an Act of Parliament. The very first official enclosure act took the common from the people of Weymouth's Radipole village and awarded the land to a wealthy local sheep farmer.

After that first "test case," enclosure of commons and other publically owned lands became more and more popular amongst those who had the power to make it happen; this took thousands of acres out public use and prevented small farmers from benefitting from that "free" resource. Although from an environmental point of view, it is agreed that by combining land to make huge fields, crop yields were much greater, from the point of view of small farmers and individuals who needed that public land in order to feed their cows, pigs and sheep, it was a disaster. It made the rich richer and the poor poorer. Nowhere was this more evident than in Dorset. Where there were once large, communal open fields, land began to be hedged in and fenced off and traditional boundaries disappeared. For many small farmers, the continuation of enclosure, which accelerated in the late 18th century and continued until the early 20th century, meant they became labourers for hire to their better off neighbours rather than independent food and feed growers. And then there was the Industrial Revolution.

Captain Swing

Adding to the misery of many agricultural workers across the country, the Industrial Revolution was spreading quickly. It began with the mechanization of the loom, displacing weavers and turning them in to common labourers. But for farmers and especially for their skilled labourers, it began with the mechanisation of threshing which was one of the most important jobs on farms that specialized in growing grains.

The job of the thresher was to separate the grains from the wheat stalk, a difficult job but one that employed a lot of workers. In the late 18th century, a mechanical thresher was invented and by the end of the first quarter of the 19th century, its use was becoming more and more common, displacing farm workers as it went. Adding to that, the harvests in 1829 and 1830 were poor and left many hungry; this in turn led to protests with workers smashing farm equipment and threatening farmers with harm if they continued to use machinery instead of people on their farms. The protesters referred to their movement as "Captain Swing," probably a reference to what many believed might be their fate if caught in the protest: they could "swing" from the gallows.

The protests began in Kent in 1830 and quickly spread towards the south; farmers in Dorset were receiving threatening letters from "Captain Swing" that fall, demanding they not only stop using threshers, but also that they contribute to the cause against them by supplying the protesters with food. The local labourers threatened farmers and their equipment in Mappowder, Buckland Newton, Lulworth, Winfrith, Wool and into Weymouth at Preston, where there were a number of large farms.

The protests were short lived as the authorities stepped in and arrested the men responsible, some of whom were imprisoned, others transported to Australia and some even ended up "swinging" from the gallows.

The farm labourer's diet

In a mid-19th century study of the Southern English diet, Dorset farm labourers were questioned about what they ate on a daily basis. It did not sound any better than the workhouse diet:

After doing up his horses, he takes breakfast, which is made of flour with a little butter and water 'from the tea-kettle' poured over it. He takes with him to the field a piece of bread and (if he has not a growing family, and can afford it) cheese to eat at midday. He returns home in the afternoon to a few potatoes, and possibly a little bacon, though only those who are better off can afford this. The supper very commonly consists of bread and water…Beer is given by the master in haytime and harvest.

Setting the poor on work

I thought they'd be strangers aroun' me,

But she's to be there!

Let me jump out o' waggon and go back and drown me

At Pummery or Ten-Hatches Weir.

I thought: "Well, I've come to the Union -

The workhouse at last -

After honest hard work all the week, and Communion

O' Zundays, these fifty years past.

"'Tis hard; but," I thought, "never mind it:

There's gain in the end:

And when I get used to the place I shall find it

A home, and may find there a friend.

"Life there will be better than t'other.

For peace is assured.

THE MEN IN ONE WING AND THEIR WIVES IN ANOTHER

Is strictly the rule of the Board."

Just then one young Pa'son arriving

Steps up out of breath

To the side o' the waggon wherein we were driving

To Union; and calls out and saith:

"Old folks, that harsh order is altered,

Be not sick of heart!

The Guardians they poohed and they pished and they paltered

When urged not to keep you apart.

"'It is wrong,' I maintained, 'to divide them,

Near forty years wed.'

'Very well, sir. We promise, then, they shall abide them

In one wing together,' they said."

Then I sank - knew 'twas quite a foredone thing

That misery should be

To the end! . . . To get freed of her there was the one thing

Had made the change welcome to me. To go there was ending but badly;

'Twas shame and 'twas pain;

"But anyhow," thought I, "thereby I shall gladly

Get free of this forty years' chain."

I thought they'd be strangers aroun' me,

But she's to be there!

Let me jump out o' waggon and go back and drown me

At Pummery or Ten-Hatches Weir.

The Curate's Kindness - **A Workhouse Irony**, poem by *Thomas Hardy*

The impotent poor...

The history of the Dorset workhouse goes back to the Tudors, but their efforts to help the poor were as much a response to a growing problem with vagrancy as they were a charitable effort. The vagrancy problem came about because of changes in law that allowed people to move freely around the country, something that had been illegal during the Middle Ages. This was exacerbated by Henry VIII's Dissolution, which closed the monasteries, eliminating the monastic orders who were the principle providers of alms and other help for the poor.

The first poor law was passed in 1572 and provided for the punishment of *sturdy beggars* and for the relief of the *impotent poor*. Another poor law was passed in 1598, the Elizabethan Poor Law, which provided a compulsory poor rate, another term for a tax, the provision of local "overseers" of the relief system, and a plan for *setting the poor on work*.

Although the work provision did not specifically call for facilities to house the poor, many communities took that step. Weymouth, Melcombe Regis, Portland and other local communities built their first workhouses after the second poor law was passed and this is when the reference "poor house" was sometimes replaced with a new term, the "workhouse."

In to the 18th century, Weymouth and its neighbours needed more and more places to house the poor, mostly because of an increase in population. These were purchased or built by both local towns and villages as well as by wealthy private benefactors. By the 1770s, the problem of what to do about England's poor had become a political issue, which led Parliament to commission a survey of the country's workhouses. In 1778, local towns and villages with recognized workhouses included at least twenty-eight facilities: Burton Bradstock with twelve inmates, Charminster with twenty, Dorchester with eighty, Fordington with twenty, Lytchett Minster with fifteen, Melcombe Regis with forty-four, "St James in the Town and County of the Town of Pool" with eighty, Portesham with fifty, and Wyke Regis with twenty.

> **The Parliamentary Report on the number of Dorset Workhouses:**
>
> Beaminster (100), Blandford Forum (50), Buckland Newton (20), Burton Bradstock (12), Charminster (20), Cranborne (60), Dorchester—Holy Trinity (80), Fordington (20), Frampton (12), Gillingham (70), Haslebury Bryan (20), Lyme Regis (32), Lytchett Minster (15), Marnhull (60), Marshwood (12), Melcombe Regis (44), St James in the Town and County of the Town of Pool (80), Portesham (50), Puddletown (20), Sherborne (130), Stalbridge (50), Stockland (30), Sturminster Newton (50), Sturton Caundle (6), Tarrant Gunvil (5), Wimborne Minster (200).

Although Weymouth and Portland had at least two workhouses each, these were missing from the report, as were the smaller poor and alms houses that were supported by individual benefactors and small charitable concerns, such as Sutton Poyntz's poorhouse, known as Church House. It also left out any information about the number of people who were reliant on "outdoor" relief. These were the poor who lived elsewhere and came to the poor or workhouse during the day to eat or collect food and alms. Many of the local workhouses also provided rudimentary health care.

Making up the pay

Most of the Dorset workhouses were funded by local taxes, which meant that a minority of residents were supporting the majority of the poor, as most locals did not make enough money to pay the tax. Those tax, or rate, payers resented having to carry the burden of the poor and they pressured the masters and matrons in charge of the workhouses to find "creative" ways to spend as little as possible. Locally, between 1820 and 1830, one of those methods was cutting the cash contributions to the needy by 20%; that money was replaced with rations of course bread. Probably not coincidentally, there was a corresponding increase in crime amongst the poor during the same period, which many blamed on the cut in support. Pinching the poor relief pennies was not unique to this era, however; by the late 18th century, communities like Dorchester did not increase their support for poor families until they had more than three children. In other Dorset towns and villages, there was no allowance for children at all.

By 1834, there was renewed pressure on Parliament to do something about the growing number of poor in England; in response, it commissioned a national Poor Law Report where a local vicar's concerns were recorded. He told of cases where the overseers of the poor in his parish were misusing poor relief funds, saying they were *in the habit of sharing out the pauper labourers among the farmers, to include themselves, and of paying for the work done wholly out of the poor's rates*. Some of those dishonest farmers also paid their casual labourers, those not on relief, solely out of the poor rates. It was this kind of abuse that helped lead to more poor law legislation.

Those of Bellfield House

In about 1775, a prominent banker and oil merchant Isaac Buxton, a native of Norfolk who resided in London, began work on an elegant Georgian house built in Bellfield Park in Wyke Regis; he called it *Bellfield House*. He hired a well-known London architect John Crunden to design the Georgian mansion, which was completed in 1780. Exactly why Buxton decided to spend a great deal of money on a home so far from his business and home is not known, but it is probably for the same reasons so many wealthy people flocked to the popular Georgian seaside resort; because King George III loved it, so did the well-to-do.

Although Isaac died only a few years after the house was finished, his wife Sarah Fowell Buxton spent a lot of time there throughout her long life as did her children and grandchildren. And the grandchild who loved Bellfield the most was the same one who inherited the house from his great grandmother at her death in 1814: Thomas Fowell Buxton.

Thomas loved spending time in Weymouth. He wrote letters describing the days he and his siblings explored the coast and noted that his grandmother, who apparently was not always the easiest person to get along with, relaxed during the long holidays at Bellfield. He also noted that George III and his family were frequent dinner guests at the Buxton mansion when they were in town. Thomas' brother Charles also loved their extended stays in

Weymouth and he married a local girl called Martha Henning; sadly, Charles died young and is buried in Wyke Regis' All Saints Church cemetery.

Thomas married a Norfolk girl, Hannah Gurney, and the young couple lived in a cottage not far from Bellfield house during the first months of their marriage. Her family owned the Gurney Bank, an important financial institution of the time and her mother was a Barclay. Eventually, the Gurneys and the Barclays brought their businesses together to become Barclays Bank. Because of his love of the community, though like his father, his business interests were in London, Thomas ran for Parliament in 1818 and was elected Member of Parliament for Weymouth and Portland, a position he held until 1837. During and after his political career, he worked tirelessly for the causes he felt very strongly about and this was helped by the fact that he had married into a staunch Quaker family who also worked hard to help make the world a better place.

Thomas' sister-in-law Elizabeth Gurney Fry, whose portrait, along with Thomas', is on the back of £5 notes, still in circulation, because of their philanthropy, began her lifetime of charity by opening a Sunday school for poor children. She went on to fight tirelessly for prison reform, helping women prisoners and their children, with special focus on education for those unfortunates. Thanks to her brother-in-law Thomas, she gave evidence to Parliament about the horrible conditions in English and Scottish prisons. Thomas' other sister-in-law, Louise Gurney, was an advocate for education for all and he was also one of the founders of the Royal Society for the Prevention of Cruelty to Animals (RSPCA). It was this activist family who were likely to have been amongst the founders of the local branch of the Society for Promoting the Lancasterian System for the Education of the Poor, which worked to provide standardized education in the local area. Sir Thomas Fowell Buxton was made the *Baronet of Bellfield in the County of Dorset and of Runton in the County of Norfolk* in 1840 and died in 1845.

The other *ism*…abolitionism and the abolitionists

Thomas Fowell Buxton worked tirelessly for education and prison reform, but the cause closest to his heart was the abolition of slavery; ending the slave trade and slavery was Thomas' primary reason for becoming Weymouth's MP. Prior to his taking political office, Quakers, the backbone of the English abolitionist movement, had had to rely on public meetings to get the word out; his election to Parliament had given him the golden opportunity to reach out to the entire British public and to give him otherwise-unattainable access to the country's leadership. In 1823, he formed the Society for the Extinction of the Slave Trade, which later became simply the Anti-Slavery Society. Although the slave trade had been abolished in the UK in 1807, slavery itself was not made illegal until the bill Thomas had helped to write, the 1833 Slavery Abolition Act, was passed. This freed all slaves in the British Empire.

Even after he left Parliament, Thomas continued to work against slavery; it was not until after WWI that his name was no longer synonymous with the end of British slavery. For some reason, history forgot about him.

A family Affair

Slavery is abominably bad under its mildest manifestations. Its effect everywhere is distressing and degrading.
William Forster

William Forster was born in 1784 in Tottenham in London; his parents were devout Quakers and he became an itinerant Quaker minister, travelling around Great Britain. When he was visiting London, he toured Newgate prison; appalled by the terrible living conditions there, he contacted prison reformer Elizabeth Fry, who then took on the job of improving prison conditions. Through her, William met Anna Buxton, Thomas Buxton's sister; she was living in Weymouth and was a favourite of King George III's. William and Anna married in Shaftsbury in 1816 and moved to Bradpole, a small village near Bridport.

William used his family's influence when, after his brother-in-law Thomas Fowell Buxton had been voted into parliament, he urged him to take up the cause of slavery. His concern was the same as Thomas', that the British slave trade may have been abolished in 1807, but there were hundreds of thousands of people still living in slavery. William's brothers Josiah and Robert Forster were also avid abolitionists and they, along with brother-in-law Thomas, were key figures in the legislation, in 1838, that put an end to the British role in the entire institution of slavery.

Narrative of the Expedition

William Allen was born in Weymouth in 1792 and was well-acquainted with Thomas Fowell Buxton. He joined the navy in 1805 and made his way through the ranks, eventually becoming a rear admiral. Allen was deeply committed to ending slavery and the slave trade and led three voyages to Africa to try to help the cause. The third trip was his most illustrious command, but it also brought an end to his career. Thomas Fowell Buxton had presented the idea of sending an elaborately equipped naval expedition down the Niger River in West Africa in order to help end the slave trade. Allen commanded the ship the Wilberforce on that voyage, but they met with repeated disasters and quite a few of the abolitionists travelling with the naval contingent died during the voyage; it was an expensive failure. Upon return to England, he helped write *A Narrative of the Expedition sent by H.M.'s Government to the River Niger in 1841* about the trip and its purpose, which detailed the reasons it had failed. That did not help his case, as many blamed him for the failure.

When Allen returned to Weymouth, he was put on half-pay and then forced to retire; he died a ruined man in his hometown in 1864. Other countries were much slower than the British to end the slave trade and the hope had been that the trip would put an end to the international trade, instead it ruined Allen and led to Thomas Fowell Buxton's loss of his seat as Weymouth's MP, as well as contributing to his premature death in 1845.

Worn-out Ministers

Many of the reformers of the 19th century were not members of the Church of England, they were often non-conformists, those who since the Reformation had increasingly chosen to worship as members of various breakaway groups. Weymouth and its neighbours are an excellent example of that, especially when it came to the Methodists. The 19th century saw a huge increase in Methodism and that is evidenced by the number of churches its members, both primitive and Wesleyan Methodists, built during the 19th and early 20th centuries. It is perhaps not surprising just how popular a religion it was, given the founder of Methodism, John Wesley, had deep roots in the local communities. One of the earliest Methodist churches was established on Portland in 1746 by the Reverend Charles Wesley, John Wesley's brother, which dissolved in 1770. The movement was revived by Robert Carr Brackenbury in 1791, who paid to have a chapel built in Fortuneswell in 1793. Brackenbury was a close friend and advisor to John Wesley and though he was from a very wealthy old Lincolnshire family and attended Cambridge, he quit school to become a Methodist minister and is credited with much of the spread of the religion across England and the Channel Islands.

The local 19th century Methodist churches were divided into two groups, the primitive and the Wesleyan; these were created through a national schism in the church, which was resolved in 1932 when the two came back together and were once again referred to as simply the Methodist Church. Local Wesleyan churches included Westham, which opened in 1902, Wyke Regis, which began in 1804, Broadwey, built in 1838, East Chaldon, built in the 19th century, Osmington, which began meeting in 1847 and built its own church in 1878, Upwey's Ridgeway Church, built in 1870, Weymouth's Conygar Lane Church, built in 1805 and later moved to Maiden St, built in 1867, and Weymouth's Derby St, built in 1871 and Weymouth Park, also built in 1871. Others included Chickerell, Portesham, and Preston-Sutton Poyntz, built in 1816, but had begun meeting in the 18th century; Easton, built in 1853, with a Wesleyan school built nearby in 1878; and Fortuneswell, Southwell and Chesil also had 19th century Wesleyan Methodist churches.

Primitive Methodist churches included Long Bredy, Fortuneswell, Weston, and Weymouth St. Leonard' Road, built in 1878, and Wyke Regis, to name a few. Some of these were served by itinerant preachers, some had permanent ministers. Weymouth also had two Methodist manses, the Wesleyan on Abbotsbury Rd, then on to Russell Ave and the Primitive Methodist manse on Spring Ave, later on Mount Pleasant Ave, all built in the 19th century. Membership ranged from a few dozen to hundreds of parishioners each, and

Weymouth and Portland churches came together with Baptist and Congregationalist churches to form the Weymouth and Portland Sunday School Union, one of the groups that helped bring formal education to many of the communities' children.

The Dorset Methodist churches were the backbone of local temperance movements and many of the churches actually kept records of the parishioners who committed in writing to abstain from drinking alcohol; those records were called "abstainers' rolls." Anyone who committed to abstain signed a pledge that read: *For the sake of Christ and His Kingdom I promise by God's help to abstain from all alcoholic drinks and beverages. Please enter my name on the abstainers' Roll of the Methodist Church.*

But possibly the most curious of the local Methodist churches' causes were the **Worn-out Ministers' and Widows' Funds.**

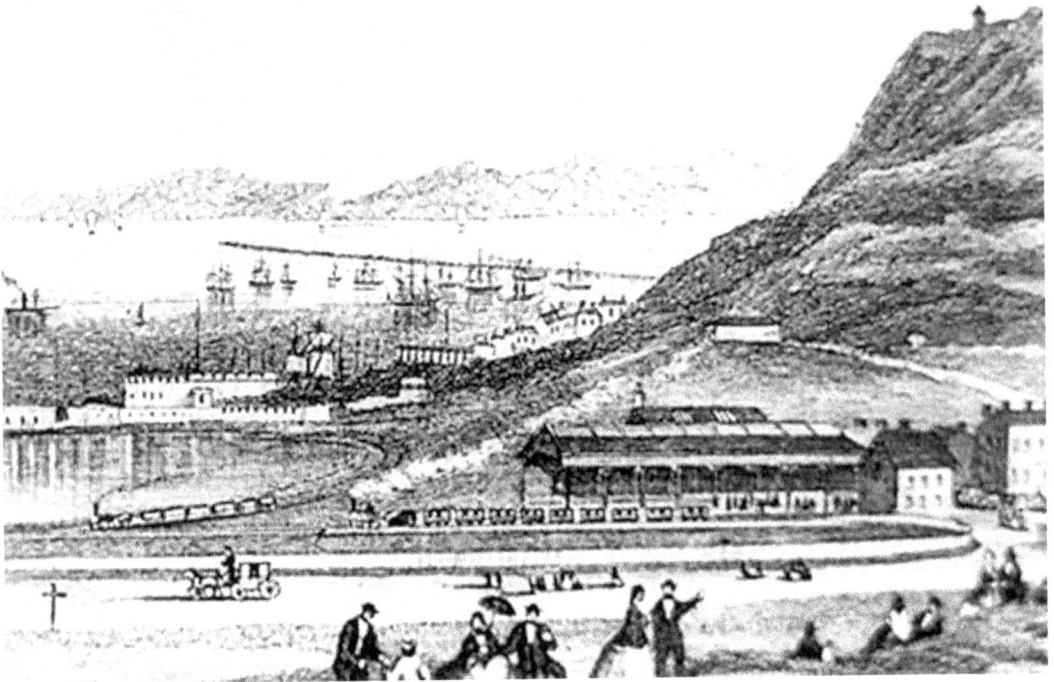

It will be the French Channel

...the billows sleep within the shelter of a wondrous pile

Of man's vast workmanship-that new made

Isle,

That marble isle-brought piecemeal form the

Shore,

To break the weltering waves, and check their

Savage roar.

Going back to at least the reign of Alfred the Great (849 – 899), Weymouth and Portland harbours were important ports of call for the Royal Navy. During his reign, Edward III built his fleet up to fight the French and he used Weymouth and its neighbours as military recruitment centres for both sailors and soldiers. Although the ports had lost some of their lustre by the late 17th century, especially as Weymouth's was not well maintained and the harbour had begun to silt up, by the end of the 18th century, especially with George III's regular presence, the Royal Navy was a constant presence. And it was this king's own clockmaker who came up with a way to make the harbours bigger and better.

Meditated Mischief

Eighteenth century clockmaker to King George III and owner of the elegant Assembly Rooms, John Harvey, was also an amateur engineer. In the 1790s, he came up with the idea of building a breakwater in Weymouth Bay and by 1813, he was working on a design he could present to the admiralty and other bodies that might be interested in his plans. In 1814, Harvey published his ideas in:

Reflections on certain facts relative to the stupendous works of Cherbourg, which have been executing at different periods of the French Government, but especially during the Tyranny of Bonaparte, for the purposes of annoyance to the Marine and Commerce of England in time of War; together with a Brief Statement of a Plan for counteracting the Meditated Mischief, by adopting similar works in Portland Roadstead. J. Harvey. Printed in Weymouth by "J. Cummins, Conygor-Lane" in 1814.

Besides the fact that a well-designed breakwater would make the ancient harbour a much safer, therefore more attractive and profitable, location for the shipping industry, the principle motivation was "Napoleon's Cherbourg." In the 1780s, a major building project had begun to create Cherbourg harbour, leading one English Admiral, Lord George Rodney, in 1787, to remark that *If Cherbourgh Harbour is completed, then the British Channel is no more; it will be the French Channel.* Over time, the work at Cherbourg required millions of pounds in labour, stone and equipment; the French built an impressive military structure, with a huge harbour connecting an enormous breakwater. Eventually, it included a massive ship building facility where dozens of vessels could be built at the same time in its huge construction bays and eighty vessels could moor inside the breakwater. The attached military barracks could house up to 8,000 soldiers at any time.

In spite of the concern over maintaining control over the English Channel and the fear over a French invasion, nothing was done to build the British equivalent of the French breakwater and harbour at what many engineering experts considered the most obvious place for an English equivalent: Weymouth and Portland harbours. In the early 1820s, Harvey reported that he had provided copies of his design to the Duke of Wellington, the Court of Admiralty, the East India Company, the Corporation of Trinity House, the Institution of Civil Engineers, and the Corporation of Weymouth, along with numerous masters of ships he felt would understand the importance of such a plan.

Finally, in 1828, those plans made the national news when a popular men's journal published an article in full support of Harvey:

But it is not to be imagined that the money necessary to supply these acquisitions to the Portland Roads, will be anything to compare with that which has been expanded on the work of Cherburgh...Although it is calculated that every yard of this structure would require 1000 tons of stone, yet there may be obtained, without any cost but that of carriage, 20,000,000 tons of waste stone...which would be enough to construct a breakwater twenty miles in extent. And as for the conveyance of it, lying as it now does, on an assent of 200 feet, over the very Bay where the works would be conducted, it might be carried thither upon an inclined railway, without the aid of either horse or engines. The owners of the quarries would be heavily glad to get rid of the encumbrance, which now covers the more marketable stone underneath, and the railway might be left for their subsequent convenience.

Mr. Harvey has dedicated his pamphlet to the Nautical and Mercantile Friends of Great Britain, and we heartily hope he may find all who have an interest in the affairs of the great sea his own friends, as well as friends to the land they live in, upon this occasion. It is in times of tranquillity and wealth that we must think of providing against the contingencies of war, as well as of establishing more firmly the blessing we already enjoy. There are poor out of number of famishing for want of employment, while the rich are in search of new pursuits whereon their hoards may be laid out to advantage. Here is an avenue before them, which, if pursued with steadiness, cannot fail to lead them to the object of their search; and in so doing, will effect other objects by the way, creditable to themselves and beneficial to their country.

It only remains to be suggested that to the town and vicinity of Weymouth the breakwater would form an incalculable acquisition; not merely as protecting their pier, their houses, their bathing-places, from hurricanes like that of November, 1824; but as presenting a noble specimen of the riches, the strength, the commerce, and the beauty of everything connected with British seamanship, and thereby enabling them to assert their title to the ranked among the first maritime stations in the world, worthy the renown of England, and the renewed presence of her monarchs.

Harbour of refuge at Portland

Actual construction began on the Weymouth breakwater in 1849, over fifty years after John Harvey had come up with the idea. The plan brought the town into the national spotlight once again, but it also started an argument over just whose idea the breakwater had actually been. National newspapers were crediting the original concept to Harvey, who had died in 1829; his son, also John Harvey, Weymouth's postmaster, had continued to put forward the claim that it had been his father's dream to see it built. Harvey, Jr. was challenged about that claim in the 1830s as national men's magazines carried a series of letters between him and an Alexander Lamb, Esq, a surveyor who claimed the breakwater had been his, not Harvey's, idea. It is difficult to tell if his claim carried some weight given it was this surveyor from Surrey who petitioned the House of Commons to build a *Harbour of Refuge at Portland* in July, 1840, almost a decade after the controversy began.

In his correspondence with the magazines, Lamb claimed that he had been in Plymouth in 1813, where there had been a meeting of various engineers examining whether *that* harbour would be a good place to build a breakwater, again in response to the "Cherbourg" threat. There was a national debate going on between various agencies as to whether there was a real need for breakwaters to be built at public expense at all. Plymouth was one of the harbours the pro-breakwater supporters were considering.

Lamb claimed that while he was there, he had been *called on by the late Christopher Idle, Esq. to accompany him to Weymouth, whither he was going as a candidate for a seat in parliament, as one of its members.* Idle was a wealthy merchant from London and one of many during the 18th and 19th centuries who did not live in Weymouth, but bought or used their influence to have their names put forward as local candidates.

THE WEYMOUTH CANDIDATES or the Strangers at Home. Plate 1

The election of 1814, when Idle was elected as MP for Weymouth and Melcombe Regis, was so corrupt, it made the national press and Idle's parliamentary record shows nothing in regards to his commitment to the community, which makes Lamb's further claims somewhat suspect. He continued his story with: *Where there, after a fatiguing morning, he proposed a ride before dinner; I suggested one to Portland. We rode over part of the island, and stopping our horses on the top of Fern Hill, were contemplating the Bay from that point of the land which commands a view of Weymouth, or more properly, Melcombe Regis. Mr. Idle asked me whether he should give the Corporation £3,000 for the purpose of repairing the Pier at North Point, then in a dilapidated state? I said, 'No: if you think of doing anything to benefit Weymouth, do that which will also benefit the country. Get a Breakwater, such as is now forming at Plymouth, run out from the shore here to the wreck of the Abergavenny, and then to the Weymouthites will not want a Pier at North Point.* Idle died long before he had time to push this plan, if it was true, but Parliamentary records do show Lamb as the petitioner for the breakwater. On the other hand, Harvey was working hard in 1813 to make the breakwater a reality, writing letters to various individuals he felt would help him push the plan. He had even drawn up a blueprint for the breakwater. Lamb even admitted in a pamphlet (published in London and sold in Weymouth) he wrote in 1849, the same year the breakwater construction began, to assert his claims, that Harvey was on the hired boat Lamb used to explore the harbours while visiting Weymouth earlier in the century, documenting the local man's direct involvement.

...of the new harbour at Portland, which, when finished, would be one of the most magnificent places of refuge in the world...

26 July, 1858, The Commons Sitting on Harbours of Refuge

Whoever came up with the original idea, in the end, it was Devon Engineer James Rendell, the designer of Brixham harbour and the breakwater at Torquay, who drew up the final design for the Weymouth and Portland breakwater. The date the building commenced was a direct response to the new artificial harbour that had just been completed at Cherbourg, making it an ever-increasing threat in the eyes of the British.

Six years before construction began on the breakwater, the Royal Commission for Harbours had voted to fund the project, citing Portland's strategic importance; its design was based on the special needs of the new and growing steam-powered Royal Navy and the accompanying defences required to protect such a vital military location. Queen Victoria and Prince Albert sailed into the harbour that year, in August 1843, and received an enthusiastic greeting from the local people. Sadly, the queen had been so sea sick on

---

The People's Money

When Rendell was chosen as design engineer, Alexander Lamb questioned his plans: Has Mr. Rendell, the eminent Engineer of the Times, shewn himself to be a fit person to be entrusted with the execution of such a work as the Breakwater in Portland Roads, on which, under his guidance, large sums (for I see, on the 1st February, 1847, he asked for £200,000) of the people's money will be expended; the work, if executed according to his plan, being comparatively valueless?

the journey from the Isle of Wight to Portland harbour, she did not leave the royal yacht, but Prince Albert was given a tour of the lower island and there were bonfires and fireworks on the Verne that evening in celebration of their visit. It was the prince's interest in the project, along with Prime Minister Sir Robert Peel's, that took the project forward after so many decades of indecision about where, when and if new breakwaters should be built in response to the "French threat."

The other reason for the breakwater

Although the reasons given for the need for a breakwater were mainly military, as the plans moved forward in the 1840s, there was another reason for building it, one that for some superseded the threat of invasion: shipwrecks. These had been a plague on merchant and military ships for centuries, as they fought the tides and the rough entry along Eastern Portland from the Channel. Even the royals experienced the problem when in 1846, on returning to the area, their yacht had to dock in Portland instead of Weymouth, because of extremely rough water. A breakwater would help create a safe haven for local and visiting ships.

Dickens' Mariner Masons

Besides the harbour's strategic military location, sitting at the base of an Isle that had been the centre of quarrying for centuries was also vital to its construction; Harvey's plan was based on using the centuries' build-up of scree piled all around the base of the Isle. He had assumed that part of the build would be free with the exception of collecting and moving it, making Portland that much more attractive. Though it was not a viable idea in the end, stone quarries were not in short supply on Portland and did supply the millions of tonnes required.

In order to provide those millions of tonnes of stone required for building the breakwater, Rendell and the primary contractor John Towlerton Leather, who made his fortune on the project, designed a rail system built to haul the stone from the top of Portland to its base, near the docks. They also advertised for skilled workers, both craftsmen and managers, from around the UK, to move to the area. One of the first jobs those workers had to do was to begin the building of a temporary prison on Portland to house convicts brought from prisons around the country to work as free labour on the breakwater. James Rendell died in 1856, but the building of the breakwater went on for another 25 years, with Sir John Coode, who had studied civil engineering under Rendell, acting as the chief engineer. He had worked as Rendell's assistant on the breakwater from the beginning, and actually spent much more time on Portland than Rendell. Coode was in charge of the Portland Harbour works from 1856 to 1872, and went on to design harbours in South America and Australia, as well as serving as a commissioner in the planning of the Suez Canal.

In order to be able to begin to lay the stone that would act as the breakwater's "wall," Rendell shipped in huge logs that were placed on long piles also made of wood; these were fixed to the sea bed with Mitchell screws at the base of the pilings, which enabled them to be dug down into the clay bed of the sea about six to eight feet. The work required divers to direct the underwater construction, a dangerous process which took three hours per each piling. The wooden, partially submerged structure which formed the staging for the stone had to support five railway lines that extended along two miles into the harbour, where it had to withstand wind and waves. The pilings were strengthened by an innovative invention Leather had commissioned for the project; it was a pressure system that pushed a creosote-based substance into the huge logs, which helped preserve them once in the water.

The building of the breakwater attracted not just the national press's attention, but also became a major British tourist attraction. One of the most famous visitors who came to see for himself just what all the excitement was about was the writer Charles Dickens, whose keen observation left an important record of just how the construction worked, right down to the fact that those huge underwater pilings were constructed by *diving masons* wearing state-of-the-art diving gear, called Deane's diving dress. The Deane's consisted of leather diving suits, with rubber and copper helmets. After a few years in to the build, diving bells were also employed, yet another state-of-the-art innovation.

> **Alexander Mitchell**
>
> The Mitchell screw was an important tool invented by Irish engineer Alexander Mitchell, who used it to build the first screw-pile lighthouse. His design was vital to allowing the building of structures that had to be fixed into very wet soils, and the Mitchell screw was essential to the breakwater's construction, though the engineer and his contribution were never really credited.

Charles Dickens' description in the 17th of April, 1858, edition of his own magazine *Household Words* provides fascinating detail of the build:

We walk forward at once towards the huge staging. The pathway is lined with blocks of stone, iron rails, and timbers; here and there lies a broken pile, with the shoe and Mitchell's screw attached. [...] Up the hill to the right run the inclines; the heavy four-wagon trains rattle down them and flit by us, each with "Prince Albert" or "Prince Alfred" puffing away behind, and dashing them off rapidly to the far end of the cage. A mile of this fine stagework is complete, and one cannot do better than start off and walk the mile. A good railed passage is provided, leading between two of the five broad-gauge roads which run to the end of the inner breakwater abreast over open rafters. The large blocks of heaped stone, which at first underlie the rafters, soon become dashed with surf, and then give way entirely to the sea, which, if the day be at all fresh, will give the visitor a sprinkling. Six hundred yards from the shore the inner breakwater ends in a noble bastion-like head, rising, with smooth round sides, some thirty feet above the waves. A space of four hundred feet separates this head from its partner, the precisely similar work at the end of the outer breakwater. The staging at this point is carried out a little to the right (not passing over the heads, but swerving slightly from them) and is narrowed to three lines of road instead of five; but, upon reaching the outer limb of the work, the five lines immediately re-assemble, and go on. together all the rest of the way. This intervening piece of three-line staging is the perfect part of the whole cage. Its firm unyielding timbers will bear, almost without vibration, the forty-eight tons of the four loaded wagons, and the weight of the engine, too. The case is far different as they pass over the older timbers near the shore, which are also unsupported by the iron rods found further on, and over which the trains dance up and down as they pass, and seem to hover about the extremist limit of safe passage.

From the point where the five lines reassemble, the whole course is free from interruption to the further end. It is a scene of bustle. Here, we pass a gang of men preparing timber for the shores and brackets that support the road-pieces; there, we see a man running along the narrow footway of the workmen—a single plank laid on each side of the rails—as much at ease as if a false step would not tumble him thirty feet down into the sea, or, worse, upon the rugged rubbly heap; which, now emerging from the waves, indicates what the nature of this outer arm is hereafter to be. The inner breakwater is already being cased with dressed stone; but the outer portion is to be left—at least, according to the present estimate—as a rough slope of rubble, which will keep the sea out quite as well. Every two or three minutes comes rumbling behind us a train, with its four loaded wagons, each wagon averaging twelve tons in weight. An ordinary load consists of a large block in the centre, some two or three feet in diameter, around which are heaped fragments of smaller sizes, the whole rising to a considerable height in the wagon. It is a fine thing to watch the tipping of the rubble through the open rafters of the cage. Every wagon has a dropping-floor, slanting downwards from back to front, but with its iron-work lighter and less massive in front than behind. It is so contrived that a brakesman, with a few blows of his hammer, knocks away the check, and sets the floor free to drop; the front drops at once, because, owing to its greater depth, it is pressed by the greater weight of stone; the whole mass tumbles with a confused uproar upon the rubble-heap below, and then the heavy iron-work behind causes the floor at once to return to its natural position, in which it is immediately re-fastened. A puff or two of the engine brings each wagon in succession over the required spot; and, unless the large stone should become jammed, the whole load is tipped, and the empty train is on its way back, in less than a minute. The jamming, when it happens, is an awkward business, and men are sometimes at work for hours with picks and crowbars before some obstinate mass will slip between the iron sides. Such accidents are almost always the result of careless packing on the part of the convicts at the top of the inclines: the process being, indeed, one that demands not a little art and skill. When the rubble embankment was still below the surface, the effect of the tipping was greatly heightened by the fine hollow roar of the great plunge into the water, and by the column of spray that was dashed high into the air.[...]

As we return along the cage, we stop to watch the "travellers" at work, where masons are setting the coping-stones of casing for the inner breakwater. Two small-wheeled trucks, perhaps eight feet apart, stand on a line of rails. On a parallel line, sixty feet distant, there are two similar trucks. From all four trucks uprights rise to the height of twelve or fourteen feet, and across these uprights a platform is laid. There are four winches, one outside each upright, by which four men can move the whole machine up or down the two widely parted lines of rails which may have two or even more lines lying between them. This extensive apparatus is required for the support of a crane, but not a common crane. It has a crane that has not great arm reaching up into the air, but consists of a series of compact, well-adjusted wheels on a small stand, which can be run upon rails up and down the sixty feet of platform. Some of the travellers are made still more complete by pivots at the top of each upright, which allow one end of the platform to be wheeled a given distance along its own set of rails, without compelling any movement at the other end. This is the machine used for setting the stone of the breakwater casing. The crane will hold a block of several tons of weight neatly hewn for the cornice which is crowning the six courses of granite wall below, and grip it fast while the workmen adjust and re-adjust, enabled by this means to set with all the nicety that could be used in the adjustment of a stone weighing pounds instead of tons. A spirit-level is invariably used; and it was also employed five-and-twenty feet below the surface of the water, by the diving masons, who, in Deane's diving dress, adjusted the foundations of the splendidly built heads. Some notion may be formed of the work bestowed upon the heads, by the fact that, though four hundred feet asunder, six inches is the utmost difference between their levels. Three hundred pounds is the lowest cost of one of the large travellers.

To know what the cage is like, we should observe the work of pushing out a new bay, or tier, or row of piles, from the end of the staging. The piles, which are made in the yard, are formed of double timbers, the two beams being securely bolted and tree-nailed together. The pieces are scarfed: that is, cut so as to overlap and be joined even or flush, and the whole pile is in section fourteen inches by twenty-eight. As soon as it is made, each pile is thrust into an airtight cylinder, and, the air both from the cylinder and the pores of the wood being extracted by means of an exhaust pump, creosote is introduced instead of air. A considerable pressure is put on, until the wood has absorbed the right number of pounds of creosote to the hundredweight. Trussed booms of at least sixty feet in length (huge rafters with perpendicular pieces fixed beneath), are now rigged out from the present staging, one boom from the centre of each road, making five in all. Each boom projects thirty feet overboard, that being the distance at which the next bay of piles is to be constructed. They are kept from swaying out of the proper direction by long pieces of timber, some six inches square, fixed to their outer end and to a point on the present staging.

The booms being thus provided for, the piles are next towed out, with cast-iron weights attached to the ends, in addition to the shoe and the Mitchell's screw, with which they are to be screwed eight feet into the ground. The ends, in consequence, sink; and the heads are hoisted up into the jaw, or forked opening formed in the outer ends of the booms. Thus the piles are held in position over the spot of ground to which they must be screwed. Capstan heads are on the heads of the piles, into which capstan bars are now put, having on the end of each a small jaw or bird's-mouth, to bite the rope when inserted. Wheeled-platforms, called trollies, are then run up to the head of the staging, and fixed there. Each trolly has a crab mounted, and firmly bolted upon it; that is, a set of winding machinery, with a barrel, and winch, and spur-gear, increasing the power and communicating motion from the winch to the barrel. Men are stationed at the crab, and as soon as they commence winding, motion is given to the capstan-bars, and by them to the pile, which is thus firmly screwed into the ground. Crossheads, of double timbers like the piles, are now fitted into their upper ends, which are formed so as to receive them, and the whole is securely bolted through. Long cranes of thirty-feet gauge are used to drop these crossheads into place. Tie-rods are also put through the piles just above the level of low water mark, to give them a greater degree of firmness, Trussed road-pieces made in the yard can now be fitted athwart the crossheads, one on either side of each pile; other timbers, called transoms and chocks, for securing the roadway in its true position, are fitted in, and the narrow plank for the workman's footway is attached to either side, and supported by brackets. The cost of making and fitting every single pile is about seventy pounds; and not less than twelve or thirteen hundred constitute the staging as it now exists. The general width of the breakwater staging where five roadways run is one hundred and fifty feet; and the length of the piles at the outer end ninety feet, exclusive of shoe and screw, thus allowing, in ten fathom water, thirty feet clear above the level of low water of ordinary, spring tides. We have seen that the staging between the two heads, where three roads only run, is steadier and less yielding to the weight of the wagons than that on either side of it, but especially near the shore. This arises from the outside pile only being trussed and stayed in the bay or row of five piles, whereas in the rows of three all the piles are supported thus; each pile is further strengthened by screw moorings, that is, by long rods of iron reaching from the head of the timbers, and screwed into the ground at a considerable angle.

Chequers

Projects connected to the breakwater were added to the original plans and some aspects of those building works went on in to the 20th century. Just a year after Rendell's death, fortifications of the harbour were added to the design. This was in direct response, once again, to what the British government believed was a renewed threat by the French; their navy had built its first ironclad and Cherbourg harbour's facilities continued to be expanded. The two greatest concerns were the potential destruction of shipping and the possibility of an enemy landing at Weymouth or Portland. The new plans included forts built on the breakwater itself, the largest and most imposing being Breakwater Fort, originally called Fort Head, but now referred to as Chequers Fort, which is probably a reference to its original camouflage pattern. The building, which was clad in steel armour and constructed on a concrete base, cost more than £200,000 (almost £9 million in today's money), the original budget of the breakwater itself.

Free from interstices

John Coode was very careful when planning the building of Chequers Fort, specifying exactly which building materials to use. He sent the engineer in charge of the project a letter which documents just how involved Coode was in the details of the building and just how important it was to get the quarrying of the stone just right and how important it was to organize the use of the railroad getting the stone to the growing breakwater: *No material to be loaded into wagons except the flint beds and clean rubble, clean quarry chippings, and grit, free from all admixture of earth and soil. The largest stones for this purpose must not exceed two tons, but when stones of this size are sent, they must not be more than one 'craned' or heavy stone in each wagon. When stones of one ton to one-half ton each are sent, they must not be more than two 'craned' or heavy stones in each wagon. The remainder of the load in each case to be made up with rubble, sprawls and chippings of all sizes, from stones of 2 cwt. Each down to fine grit, mixed in such proportions as will make the mass compact and free from interstices…The wagons containing this special foundation material must be sent to the weigh-bridge in separate trains and marked with a distinguishing plate.*

There were various plans for the fort, the first by Coode in 1859, but it was eventually agreed upon that a plan drawn up by Royal Engineer Captain E.H. Steward was the most practical; the building was completed in the early 1870s and was one and a half miles from Portland's port. It could house up to 30 soldiers and was heavily armed, to include a section of the basement fitted out in the early 1890s to house torpedoes, a new weapon at the time.

Palmerston's Follies

Chequers Fort was one of a series of iron clad forts built in the 1860s; they were often referred to as Palmerston's Follies because though the Royal Commission on the Defence of the United Kingdom voted in 1860 to have them built, the forts took so long to complete that by the time they were finished, the French threat was over. That country was busy fighting the Franco-Prussian War and did not have the time or resources to fight the British, too.

Because military technology was moving very quickly by the 1860s and 70s, the fort's guns became obsolete very quickly; though Portland's artillery was updated into the 20th century, the expensive maritime forts were also obsolete before they had seen any action. This is why they became known as "Palmerston's Follies," because Lord Palmerston, who was Prime Minister in 1860, had used his position to push for their construction, which turned out to be an expensive yet pointless project.

The South Fort

A British Medical Journal article from the 1860s discussed the problem of Cholera, specifically amongst the military, and the government plans to set up separate hospital facilities for sufferers. That exchange provides a snap shot view of one of the lessor forts built on the breakwater, South Fort:

FORTS AND HOSPITALS. We see it stated, 'that the Admiralty have it in contemplation to convert the first of the series of forts now in course of completion on the Portland Breakwater into a hospital, to be used for the sick in the naval (and military) forces that may be from time to time stationed at Portland. A healthier spot,' it is added, 'could not have been selected. The South Fort of the Breakwater is situated about a quarter of a mile from the main land, and is nearly surrounded by the sea.' We think there is some misapprehension about this. The works on the Breakwater being now completed, it has been under consideration whether some of the buildings which were employed as offices, etc., during the period of its construction, might not be made available for temporary sick quarters for the Channel Fleet when that squadron is at Portland. These offices are on the land, and not on the Breakwater. This matter is under consideration, we believe. The forts on the Breakwater are casemated structures, and, ipso facto, entirely unfitted for sick people-scarcely fit for the residence of healthy persons.

Other lessor buildings on the breakwater itself included a small two-storey house at the south western end. It was made of Portland stone and had an iron roof; built in the early 1850s, it was intended to house the overseer of the construction works. Getting to and from work must have been quite interesting.

The Nothe

The Nothe Fort, though not located on the man-made breakwater, was also built as part of the harbour defences; it was constructed on the Nothe peninsula, where there had been a Neolithic hill fort and later, a Civil War fortification, all traces of which were destroyed when the land was being prepared for the new building. Standing just behind this fort was the series of Georgian military barracks that had played such an important role during the Napoleonic Wars. This fort was begun in 1860, with a sea wall built first in order to allow the front of the peninsula to be levelled off for construction. The Royal Commission approved the plans for a casemented fort, made out of Portland stone, but a few years in to the build, the contractor went out of business. In 1862, the 26 Company Royal Engineers took on the work, using mostly convict labour to complete the project. The plans included a drawbridge and portcullis to protect the timber; an iron bullet-proof gate, popular in the building of castles for thousands of years; and a ditch caponier, an extended entry which helped the defenders keep anyone trying to enter the fort from breaching its walls. It was constructed on three levels and had seventy rooms in total. The first soldiers garrisoned in the Nothe were from the Tatton-Browns, a battery of the Royal Artillery. The building was fully commissioned in 1871.

The Verne Citadel

Designed in part by another Royal Engineer, Captain W. Crossman, in 1857, with some modifications done by the Royal Commission in 1859, the Verne Citadel, by far the largest building included in the breakwater development, eventually encompassed over 56 acres and was part of one of the biggest earthworks in English history and like the Nothe, it too was built over an ancient hill fort. The project included moving millions of tonnes of stone from the Verne in order to build the breakwater, which had begun ten years before. The removal of stone around the site of the Citadel created a dry moat and a sharp incline at its entrance.

Like the Nothe, the Verne was designed with caponiers and a drawbridge at the main entry, but this was a much bigger and more complex facility. The plan was to build a fort that would accommodate the troops who would defend the breakwater and the naval and shipping interests around Portland and the harbour; it was designed to be impregnable to outside attack. The accommodations were extensive, with enough living area and supporting facilities for eight officers and 484 soldiers, expanded later to house over a 1,000 men. It also included a gym, recreation areas, a tennis court and cricket grounds, as well as kitchens, bathing facilities, a tailor's shop, a sergeants' mess, a guardroom and even its own small prison. There were also storage rooms for bedding, meat, coal, bread and other foods, as well as for utensils. The hill itself had been excavated to create a huge underground facility. At the centre of the compound, there was a huge parade ground. There were also extensive blocks of accommodation for officers and military families and bachelor quarters and cottages for specialist staff. Nearby and accessible via open passages from the Citadel, batteries that housed massive guns pointed out to sea and toward the harbour were built, ready to fire on an invading force.

The Grove Convict Establishment

The first sixty-four convicts who were brought to Portland to work on the breakwater arrived on a steamer in Castletown, at the base of Portland harbour, in November 1848. Many of them would have begun their prison sentences in solitary confinement at Millbank Prison in London. Their first task, along with the hundreds of others who followed, was to build their own prison. Preliminary building works had already begun in an area on the Eastern side of Portland, not far from the Verne, known as the Grove. It hugged the cliffs above the sea and was a very bleak place to have to work and live, especially for men unused to such an environment.

As the work continued on the breakwater, the prison camp was expanded in the 1860s to house a prison work force that continued to grow as the breakwater project grew. Over the life of the breakwater and related construction, thousands of prisoners came and went from the prison; the whole plan, when the decision was made to use prison labour, was to divert prisoners from all over Britain to work first on the breakwater, then to be transported to Australia. The assumption was that by offering the men a shortened final sentence in Australia, or even their freedom once they arrived, they would cause no trouble and would work hard.

As well as the actual prison, which was formally dubbed the Grove Convict Establishment, the prisoners also had to build the facilities that supported it; kitchens, blacksmith shops, wash rooms, barber shops (where every prisoner had his head shaved on a regular basis), even a room for the chains some prisoners were forced to wear while they worked. Most of these were outbuildings. The prison even had its own quarry within its walls; the stone the convicts produced went to build the breakwater and its buildings as well as the prison itself. Eventually, they also helped construct a gas works and a reservoir, as well as a road to the village of Easton. The prison even had its own farm.

Pentonville

Portland was one of three "model" penitentiaries built between 1848 and 1850; the others were Dartmoor and Pentonville. These were designed to be organized and productive, rather than model the filthy and degraded conditions of other prisons of the times, but they were also structured to keep the men isolated and to punish them with pointless, extremely hard labour. There, Portland differed, as the work was very hard, but the quarrying and building of the breakwater and its structures were considered vital to national security.

St. Peter's Church

Another construction project carried out by the prisoners was their own church, St. Peter's, which was built of Portland Stone and completed in 1875. As with many of the buildings on Portland, much of the work was done by convicts from the prison. The mosaic in the church was made by Constance Kent; although she did not do her time at the Grove, she was also a convict. She had been found guilty of murder when she was twenty and served twenty years in prison where she learned how to make mosaics. She is quite well known for her church mosaic work, to include one she designed for St. Paul's Cathedral. Other mosaic work in the chapel was also done by women prisoners and the furniture, lectern and pulpit were made by Grove prisoners. The chapel was consecrated in August 1872 and was designed by Major-General Sir Edmund Du Cane when he was the chairman of the convict prison directories and surveyor-general of prisons. The cost of the build was £8000, almost £366,000 today.

Although the workers were "free" labour, their prison was not; the original budget to build it was £50,000, about £2,200,000 in today's money. Unfortunately, the plan had not actually been approved by Parliament. That was a problem because the original builder, a Peter Thompson from London, spent his own money to get the project started, but had received no compensation within the first two years of its building, destroying his business in the process. That did not stop construction, however, and the prison was eventually completed, and continued to expand. After the breakwater was finished, the decision was to keep the prison open and a bigger facility was built out of Portland stone on the same site.

An unusual sort of tea room

Like Charles Dickens, there were many tourists who travelled to Weymouth and Portland to see the amazing sights provided by the building of the breakwater, but that was not the only attraction. Portland's prison also became a mecca for the curious and perhaps the ghoulish, who loved watching the prisoners working in their quarry. Enterprising local women realized the potential to profit from this curiosity; those who were "lucky" enough to live in the accommodations which ran along the walls of the prison quarry, which had been built to house prison employees, advertised their upstairs parlors as tea rooms, where the visitors could sit sipping away, watching the prisoners toil; unique entertainment for a unique place.

Who were they?

The seemingly never-ending supply of prisoners to the Grove coincided with a dramatic increase in the English crime rate; in 1800, there were 5000-recorded offences in Great Britain. In 1840, there were 20,000. Prior to 1787, many 18th century prisoners were shipped off to the American colony of Georgia, but after the American Revolution, Australia became the dumping ground for English prisoners. A total of 160,000 were transported up to the 1850s, when legitimate immigrants to Australia began to complain about having so many prisoners sent there. The imprisoned included men, women and children as young as nine. The prisoners who were sent to Portland were all able-bodied men who took part in the new "model" penitentiary system; this too was part of the transport scheme, but before they were taken to Australia, they had to work very hard; part of the answer as to why these men did not just give up and refuse to work is in the innovative system of rewards – as opposed to punishments – a few prisons began to implement, using positive rather than negative incentives.

Although it differed from prison to prison, Portland was one of a number of 19th century facilities that used a system of badges to keep track of each prisoner's length of service and behaviour. They noted the number of years the man had been sentenced, how many months he had already served and a reference to his behaviour. Here, the 7 meant that the prisoner had been sentenced to *seven* years' transportation; the 8, that he had been in prison for 8 months, and the V. G. meant that he been *very good* throughout the time he had been there.

The badges were collected once every month and taken to the governor's office, where the prison "character-book" was kept; this contained weekly reports about convict behaviour from the warders, the term used to describe the Grove's prison guards. The badges were altered according to that information and given back to the prisoners. If they had behaved badly, they lost some of the privileges they had earned from previously good conduct.

A national study done in the late 1850s of some of Britain's prisons reported it this way: *The badges which are given as a record to the prisoner of his actual position with reference to character, have proved to be a great encouragement; and that they are prized is evidenced by the efforts made to obtain them, and to regain them by good conduct in such cases as they may have been forfeited.* And the Governor of Portland Prison put it this way:

The system of wearing conduct-badges on the dress, by which the monthly progress of each convict towards the attainment of his ticket-of-leave is publicly marked, works very satisfactorily, as is evidenced by the anxiety of even the ill-conducted prisoners to regain a lost good-conduct mark, and the efforts to keep subsequently clear of the misconduct book.

As a means of promoting good conduct, a system of classification has also been adopted, the object of which will be best understood from the rules established with reference to it, which are as follows: The prisoners shall be divided into three classes, to be called the first, second, and third classes. The classification shall depend, in the first instance, on the report of character arid general conduct since conviction that nosy be received with a prisoner; and subsequently, on his actual conduct, industry, and observed character under the discipline of the establishment.

Prisoners in either the first or second classes shall be liable to removal to a lower class for misconduct. The prisoners in the different classes shall be distinguished by badges, indicating the particular class to which each prisoner may belong. Prisoners who habitually misconduct themselves will be liable to be sent back to separate confinement, or to be removed to some penal establishment under more severe discipline.

The object of the classification is not only to encourage regularity of conduct and a submission to discipline in the prison, by the distinctions that will be maintained in the different classes, but to produce on the mind of the prisoners a practical and habitual conviction of the effect which their own good conduct and industry will have on their welfare and future prospects. Such distinctions shall be made between the classes, and such privileges granted, as shall promote the object of giving encouragement to those whose good conduct may deserve it, provided such distinctions do not interfere with discipline nor with the execution of a proper amount of labour on public works.

Report on the Discipline and Construction of Portland Prison, and its connection with the System of Convict Discipline now in operation, by Lieut.-Col. Jebb, C.B., 1850.

What the governor meant by privileges was that food was often used as a reward – or punishment, as in a bread and water diet – as was tobacco, alcohol, shorter working hours, even cash incentives found a place in the prisons of the 1850s and 60s, but as advanced as some of this may sound, Portland's prison was not necessarily any less violent a place than any other prison; part of that was the nature of such a place, where pent up men often fought bloody battles over food, drink or tobacco.

Portland's prisoners were not usually isolated in the same way those in other 19th century prisons were, mainly because the work they did was not solitary, but they did have to wear uniforms that set them apart from one another, creating a kind of pecking order. Some even had to work in chains; these were the men warders considered serious flight risks. Anyone labelled as a "ruffian" had to wear grey and yellow to indicate he too was possible trouble. The prisoners who wore grey and black were assumed to be of a violent nature and were also watched very closely. The guards had good reason to fear these men; there were quite a few murders committed especially by the convicts in grey and black, most of their victims' warders, though prisoner-to-prisoner violence was not uncommon either. Some fights were allowed to go on in order to diffuse tension, to provide entertainment or simply because the warders were fearful of getting hurt themselves. In 1873, for instance, a prisoner died of a fractured skull *caused by one prisoner kicking another on the temple during a quarrel.* In fact, the 1870s seemed to be the most violent decade, with many assaults listed in the prison records. In 1878, there were 87 violent prisoner-against-prisoner assaults; in 1879, that was down to 79 and by 1880, it was down to 43. The governor of the prison blamed it on trafficking in food and tobacco.

Considered themselves ill used

The model system may have been quite effective, but there were many incidents throughout the 19th century that demonstrated what a dangerous place Portland prison could be. Not long after its opening, the Criminal Act of 1853 was passed. That act was updated in 1857; this version included a provision for shortening the sentences of those men who worked hard and had behaved well during their imprisonment. That meant that the men who were convicted between 1853 and 1857 had no hope of a shortened sentence, no matter how hard they worked or how well they got along with their fellow prisoners. This led to a serious disturbance in 1858, when 300 prisoners refused to work; the governor blamed the problem on *that they considered themselves ill used in having no remission of sentence for good conduct such as the men under the Act of July 1857 had.* Apparently, the prisoners were so aware of the difference in their statuses, those sentences under the 1857 law taunted the others, which led to constant friction.

Who were they?

The census of 1871 gives a glimpse of who was living and working at the Grove; there were nineteen warders and assistant warders, with only five of those from Dorset and only one of those from Portland. Of the nineteen men, only three were married; their wives and children would have lived at the Grove in the quarters that had been built for the warders and their families. The other sixteen lived in the single's quarters, a system similar to the military.

There were 900 prisoners and of those, only one man was from Weymouth, with no prisoners from Portland; he was 38, unmarried and called himself a "marine store dealer," which in the 19th century could have been a legitimate seller of equipment related to shipping or a junk dealer. There is no way to know which this prisoner, John Bowers, was. Like the warders, few of the other men were from Dorset; just six, who came from Cranborne, Sherborne, Cattistock, Dorchester and two from Bridport. There were even prisoners from France, Holland, the United States and Germany and almost nine percent of them came from Ireland.

Prisoner "professions"

The majority of prisoners were listed as labourers, but there were quite a few colliers, painters, miners, marines, seaman, soldiers, clerks, gardeners, tailors, smiths, bakers and even a policeman. Those professions are recognizable today, but there were dozens of men whose professions have disappeared from the modern workforce. There was an iron turner, who turned metal on a lathe, and a whipmaker who made horsewhips. The puddler turned cast iron, brass and bronze castings, the lighterman operated a flat-bottomed boat used to load and unload ships and the button turner made buttons by hand. The hemp dresser worked in the fabric industry using a hackle, a type of comb that separated the course part of the flax in preparation for weaving the fabric in to linen. The blacking maker made shoe black by mixing tallow and lamp black and the coal higgler would have gone around with a barrow selling pieces of coal for kitchen ovens and household stoves; and the jet worker formed and buffed jet found along the northern coast, cutting it into shapes that could be mounted in jewellery.

Then there was the rag and bone man, who went from road to road, calling just that "rag and bone" as he hauled his load of other peoples' unwanted rags and animal bones, hoping to collect enough to sell to the paper industry. There were also the men whose professions may no longer exist in the local area, but seem quite obvious: the chair mender, caneworker, letter stamper, cotton spinner, silk winder, stone cracker, hatter, slater, book edge guilder, boot closer, forgeman, bleacher, draper, bottler and dyer. And the most interesting of them all? Under professions, one of the convicts had declared himself a "thief."

Winners and losers

For all the excitement and suspense, the building of the breakwater and its supporting facilities caused around Britain, it was not without its tragedies and its victims. The long breakwater, while under construction, offered another obstacle during heavy storms to the many ships coming and going from the harbour; dozens were wrecked on the structure, adding to the long list of centuries' worth of shipwrecks on the Dorset coast. The storms also claimed extensive lengths of the breakwater staging before its completion, adding to the costs and putting lives at risk. The breakwater railroad experienced a number of accidents, with waggons and trucks leaving the tracks and falling in to the sea, along with their cargo, and often, the men riding in them.

The incline of the inland rail that brought stone from the quarries had its share of accidents, when the very steep incline from the isle to the port meant waggons or operators lost their grip and "ran away," killing anyone in their path. As the breakwater was built in sections, each part of it was at risk during the initial laying of the pilings. During a storm in 1858, a number of pilings were washed away, its logs found scattered along the local coastline. There was also a fire in one of the temporary wooden lighthouses, which burned down to its base. The greatest human loss was of the labour force, both free and convict; some were crushed by large stones during the process of breaking up the stone, others while moving it or putting it in place. Some of the men drowned and others were mortally wounded by the large equipment they had to use to quarry and move the stone from quarry to site.

What about the locals?

Going back to the Celts, much of Portland's land was used for public grazing and many of its fields were also shared space. When changes were made in land use or other areas of island life without the permission of its traditional local ruling body, the Court Leet, the perpetrators were held to strict account. But, when the Royals put their stamp of approval on the breakwater project and all other bodies involved followed suit, life on the isle would never be the same again, as much of the common land was taken over for quarrying and building the Verne and the prison.

When the work on the huge project was in the planning stages, the Leet tried to assure the continued rights of Portlanders; meetings were held, some of which attracted crowds of hundreds, even thousands, of people, to discuss what they might do about this unprecedented land grab of traditionally shared space. When it was accepted that the local people could not prevent the government from taking their land, a final meeting was called, the purpose being to elect a group of local men to negotiate the matter of how Portlanders were going to be compensated by the government. Although many locals simply wanted their representatives and the Leet to say "no" to the demands, wiser heads realized it was not a matter of "yes or no," and there was little point in fighting the inevitable; it became a matter of how much money they would get and how it would be distributed.

The final amount agreed was £20,000, just under £1,200,000 in today's money. And then the wrangling began. The Portland leaders decided that landowner tenants, farmers who owned and worked their own land, would receive half of the money, and the rest was used to construct public works and to assure Portlanders would no longer have to pay the toll when they travelled between the isle and Weymouth; the toll booth, located in Wyke Regis at the Fleet, was built in the 18th century and the county leased out the rights to charge travellers who wanted to go through to Weymouth or back to Portland. Prior to the Portland-Breakwater agreement, that toll booth was so lucrative, two armed guards were on watch at all times, the only Dorset booth with such an arrangement.

The other building boom

In response to the need to house the many labourers working on the breakwater, there was a rush to build houses on Portland, especially in the Underhill area. In 1841, there were 567 single homes and just over 2,800 people on the Isle; in 1851, there were 786 single homes and almost 8,470 people.

Prior to the arrival of a huge number of prisoners, skilled and semi-skilled labourers flocked to Weymouth and Portland, and of course, local men were hired by the score. The infrastructure which supported the huge breakwater construction projects also had to be created in order to quarry the stone and deliver it to the harbour. This included laying the tracks for the railroad, as well as loading and unloading materials and equipment as they arrived and even getting a head start on building the prison. But with the arrival of the newcomers, as many as a thousand by the end of the 1840s, meant changes to the social structure of the local area, too, especially on Portland. Labourers, many of them, arrived unaccompanied, which meant custom for pubs and other businesses, but the behaviour of some of those workers disrupted the calm of island life. Then, when the prisoners began to arrive, almost half of those workers, a mix of local men and new arrivals, suddenly became redundant and were now looking for work, creating a labour force glut.

And then there was Brunel.

The Great Eastern

Although the breakwater was not complete in 1859, it was decided that since the new harbour was by then the largest man-made port in the world, it was big enough to accommodate the biggest ship in the world; no doubt the combination really appealed from a marketing standpoint. The Great Eastern was a coal-fuelled iron steam ship, designed by Isambard Kingdom Brunel, one the most famous engineers in British history. The ship carried enough coal to steam from England to Australia AND BACK AGAIN without re-fuelling and was five times bigger than anything else afloat when it was launched that year.

The plan for the Great Eastern was for the ship to begin its career as a luxury passenger ship by sailing in and out of Portland as part of its maiden voyage. Sadly, hours before her pending arrival into the port, one of the ship's funnels blew off in an explosion caused by a water heater's steam valve being closed off. The explosion was that much worse because the ship's bulkheads were so thick and well-built, the strength of the blast went up through the funnel, which killed five coal stokers who were scalded to death. Then the captain and his boy got into a rowboat and were lost at sea, and another crew member who had either fallen off or jumped overboard, was also lost to the waves and at least five others were also badly injured.

Once the ship was repaired, its original purpose was short lived - it simply was not profitable as a luxury liner — but it did have a second life as the ship that helped lay the

Atlantic underwater cable between Europe and the US, making telegraph communication possible between the two continents. And locally, the ship's story lived on in an odd way; the funnel blown over by the explosion was sold to the local water company in Sutton Poyntz and worked as a filtering device, until it found its way to a museum.

As it took some years for the admiralty to take over all of the lands they had "purchased," the impact was not felt all at once, but as much of the land went to building the Verne and creating new or expanding pre-existing quarries, life never returned to normal. Common grazing land and all the customs involved with it disappeared forever. And then there were the newcomers.

The other church

Although the Grove prison had its own prisoner-built church, there were far more people served by its neighbouring church, one that was built out of the need to serve the Catholics who came to the local area, because many of the newcomers who arrived to help build the breakwater were Catholics, which led to the need for a Catholic church on Portland. Very near the Grove prison, the Church of Our Lady and St. Andrew was built in 1868 to serve that workforce, as well as to offer services to the other local Catholics. Prior to this permanent church, a small building, also called the Church of Our Lady, adjacent to the site of the new church, had served as a chapel, probably built there at the same time the building of the Verne and the Grove began in 1848. The church was designed by Joseph Hansom, the designer of the Hansom cab.

A local priest, Father Lawrence Smythe from Weymouth, held services for the entire Catholic community, which included prisoners and warders, as well as workers, merchant mariners and military. During the same period, a mass centre was opened in a private home on Portland by Father Martin Hoskins; it was very popular with the Isle's Catholics and well attended up to the point that the permanent church was built. Mass was said on Palm Sunday of 1856 and fifty people attended, indicating what an important role these services were providing to many on Portland.

Rowdy Tourists

As the Great Eastern was being repaired in Portland harbour, the owners had the bright idea of opening it up to visitors. The many tourists who visited the area to see the breakwater and the prison also took advantage of seeing the biggest ship in the world, as did the locals, but so many people showed up – and were not necessarily very respectful - the interior was badly damaged. That damage was so extensive, the owners doubled the cost of entry to keep out the local hooligans.

The "other" Catholics

From the 1860s, Portland's Grove was the prison where hundreds of members of the Fenian Brotherhood, an Irish organization fighting for Irish independence from the British, were sent. These men were treated very differently than the average prisoner held there. Although the Irishmen were assigned their own chaplain and attended mass when warders deemed it appropriate, their treatment was often barbaric and illegal according to the laws governing prisoner treatment. The Fenians were political prisoners rather than criminal offenders, which meant they were supposed to be separated from the criminals; not only were they not separated, they were forced to clean for those other inmates, something that led to frequent attempts at causing disturbances to annoy the warders. Portland's warders responded with severe beatings, terrible and inadequate food, filthy conditions, and the withholding of medical care.

The known leaders of the Fenians were treated the worst; one of those, O'Donovan Rossa, who served many years at Portland, was held in solitary confinement for months at a time and at one point, the guards handcuffed his hands behind his back for 35 days, during which he had nothing to eat or drink but bread and water. He was so disliked that the governor of the prison spread a rumour that Rossa *did carry on an intrigue with the wife of another prisoner,* a rather sad attempt to divide and conquer the Irishmen, who always seemed to find ways to communicate with one another, something that frustrated the warders and the governor. One of those who worked to disrupt prison life included John Devoy, one of the organizers of the Fenians, who while imprisoned at Portland encouraged his fellow Irishmen to strike out against their terrible treatment, which just got him transferred to another prison. Even Karl Marx, who was very interested in the Irish fight for freedom, noted their terrible treatment at Portland's prison. The Fenians who were held in the 1860s were amongst the very last group of prisoners who were transported to Australia;

in October 1867, the same ship that had brought the first prisoners to Portland, the Hougoumont, was loaded with 280 convicts, 62 of them Fenians.

Royal visits

From this spot on the 25th of July 1849 his Royal Highness Prince Albert consort of Queen Victoria sank the first stone of this breakwater. Upon the same spot Albert Edward, Prince of Wales, on the 18th of August 1872 laid this last stone and declared the work complete. These are imperial works and worthy kings.'

Queen Victoria and especially Prince Albert had shown a tremendous interest in the breakwater and many believed it was that interest and support that made the project happen, or at least pushed it forward at a faster rate than it might have done without that royal backing. They visited in 1843, 1846, and 1849, always arriving to great enthusiasm by the local residents and visiting military. Prince Albert continued to be fascinated with the Breakwater project until he died in 1861, the same year he visited Portland without the queen. His yacht, the Prince Consort, arrived on the 8th of August and he was accompanied on this trip by his son Prince Arthur and his daughter Princess Victoria, along with her husband Prince Frederick Wilhelm of Prussia, who became Frederick III, Emperor of Germany and King of Prussia, in 1888.

"On the 25th day of July, A. D., 1849, in the 12th Year of the reign of Her Most Gracious Majesty,

QUEEN VICTORIA,
His Royal Highness, Prince Albert,
K. G., &c.,

DEPOSITED THIS STONE,
TO RECORD THE COMMENCEMENT OF

THE PORTLAND BREAKWATER.

JAMES MEADOWS RENDEL, Engineer in Chief,
JOHN COODE, Resident Engineer."

Leaving the royal women behind, the men went up the incline to view the fortifications at the Verne and at East Weare. They were fascinated by the entire works, visiting the batteries, roads, and magazine excavations. Then they went down the incline to see the section of tracks that circled the Verne.

Sadly, Albert died the same year as that visit, but his son Prince Albert Edward came back to the community in 1872. That year, the first two arms of the breakwater were completed and there was a huge celebration on the 10th of August to mark the occasion. The prince and his wife Princess Alexandra of Denmark, took part in the ceremonies which included a huge flotilla of the Royal Navy Channel and Reserve Squadrons, led by the navy's new broadside ironclads including the Minotaur, Agincourt, Achilles and Hercules; all of the sailors and officers on board sailed past the royals and saluted their welcome hello to the family.

The country's largest construction project to date had caused the deaths of hundreds of workers and passers-by, had irrevocably altered the natural environment of the harbour and of course, Portland, but it had also changed the whole nature of that Isle. Even with the arrival of Christopher Wren, when Portland stone was used for the rebuilding of much London after the great fire of 1666, and all that entailed, had seen Portlanders remain true to their ancient ways of life. Even after the completion of the breakwater and the exodus of many workers, the changes and the arrival of newcomers did not stop. The world's largest man-made harbour was one of the busiest in the world; throughout the rest of the century, it would have been rare to have seen fewer than 200 ships in and around the harbour, most Royal Navy vessels. This simply increased as time went on. The final phase of the breakwater was completed in 1906, with two more arms enclosing the harbour. These were added as more protection against foreign attack.

Portland or Dartmouth?

Portland became home to the Royal Navy's Channel Fleet, which had been created to protect the Channel from the French in the 1690s. Its importance grew as Cherbourg's harbour grew. When the breakwater was still under construction, the naval training ship The Brittania made the harbour its home in 1862. Portland remained its home until 1865, when the decision was made to move the training of naval officers to Dartmouth, where it remained. The reasoning for the move was based on the problematic weather and tides that had made shipping difficult for centuries; Dartmouth was far more protected, safer for the training of "our future admirals." Portland did remain an important location for some of the naval training, however; for forty years, there were a series of training ships that were based in the harbour. All of those ships had the same name: HMS Boscawen.

The art and artists of Weymouth and its neighbours: The Mssrs. Prout, Turner, Constable, Upham and Pye

Weymouth and its neighbours were favourite locations for a number of important artists of the 19th century. Some of them chose to live in the community, others found their inspiration on visits to the area. All of them found the beautiful coastline a powerful muse, whether in golden sunshine or pouring rain.

Samuel Prout is considered one of the greatest English watercolour artists of the 19th century; he was also one of the first to explore lithography and was known around Britain and Europe for his use of light and shade. Although he was born in Norfolk in 1783, he was educated in Plymouth, which introduced him to the West Country, and though Prout travelled all over Europe, creating beautiful works of art as he went, one of his greatest inspirations was the Dorset coastline, which he discovered when he lived in Weymouth, where he remained for fifty years, moving to the area after falling in love with the community and its neighbours during his West Country travels. Portland was one of his favourite subjects, with its fishermen's cottages, fishing boats and rugged beauty.

Joseph Mallord William Turner was born the son of a barber in London in 1775. Some art experts called him one of England's finest artists and he became known as the *painter of light*. He exhibited at the Royal Academy from 1790 until his death in 1851.

Like other artists of his time, he was a Romantic painter, but he was not just an artist who followed this art movement, he was one of its founders. Turner travelled extensively throughout Europe looking for inspiration, but he also loved the Dorset coast, where he stayed in Weymouth and Lyme Regis, using the seaside as his inspiration during his visits.

John Constable was born in Suffolk in 1776 and he was yet another Romantic painter, principally known for his landscapes. He was inspired by the Dorset coast during his honeymoon in Osmington in 1816. He and his wife Maria Elizabeth were invited to stay in the village by their friend, a local man, the Reverend John Fisher, whose uncle, also John Fisher, was the Bishop of Salisbury and had married the couple. The reverend owned a home in the village and introduced Constable to the beauties of the local villages and coastline; he was also an avid painter and may have painted beside the artist as they created very similar images of Osmington Village. Although Constable did n5ot become a member of the Royal Academy until he was 52, and was never very successful financially, his paintings sold well in France and his most famous local image of Weymouth beach was exhibited in a number forms and was quite well known in the art community. He died in 1837.

John William Upham was born in Honiton, Devon in 1772, but moved to Melcombe Regis sometime in the late 18th century. He was a both a painter and engraver and painted mostly landscape scenes of his community and around Dorset, but he also travelled to Europe where he painted scenes of Switzerland. He created paintings that were turned into engravings and sold together in bound publications to locals and tourists visiting Weymouth, where he died in 1828 in Weymouth. Upham exhibited at the Royal Academy as did the other artists who have left a visual record of what Weymouth and its neighbours looked like in the early part of the nineteenth century, and he is sometimes called a *Professor of Drawing, Weymouth*, but it is difficult to determine just what that title entailed and where and who he taught.

The artist William Pye was born in Blackburn, Lancashire in 1855. In the 1880s, he moved to Weymouth, where he lived for 50 years. While he was a local resident, he exhibited at the British Institute, the Royal Society of British Artists and the Royal Academy. When he died in 1934, the newspaper the Southern Times said *Mr. Pye did much to put Dorset on the map in the art world, the variety of the county proving an endless source of inspiration to him and his brush has recorded virtually every scene of interest on the Dorset coastline.*

Transport: Turnpikes and Tolls

Transportation in early Britain had been a haphazard affair; rough tracks were the only way to travel by horse and wagon and most people would have travelled on foot, along paths designed to move farm animals from one place to another. Though the Romans had laid important roads, they were not evenly distributed throughout the country and during the Middle Ages, those were not well maintained because there was no central government, meaning no one to take responsibility for organizing the repair and extension of them.

As most areas of the country were quite isolated and the average Briton was unlikely to ever travel more than twelve miles outside of his place of birth, the limited roads were not a huge problem, even less so because over 90% of the population would not have owned a horse, let alone a wagon. All that changed in the Elizabethan era, which was a time of tremendous financial expansion leading to a need for better transport. Even though many towns and cities were empowered by acts of Parliament to conscript locals to work on road extensions and maintenance, it was both an unpopular move and difficult to enforce, meaning improvements were limited.

In another attempt to solve the growing transport problems, in the 1650s something akin to toll roads were introduced around the country in order to help pay for building new ones and maintaining old ones. This, again, did not help keep up with the growing economy and the number of vehicles that had made that growth possible, so a formal system of turnpikes was introduced by act of Parliament in the 1660s. It began with the Great North Road (today's A1) which ran from London to York and on to Edinburgh and was used primarily by the mail coaches. In the first decade of the 18th century, this expanded with turnpike trusts, created to help further road building, as well as to establish standards in road building and maintenance. Part of this big plan were the toll houses, where travellers paid the fee, or toll, to be allowed to travel on the roads.

Dorset's first turnpike was built in 1753; it ran from Wiltshire to Shaftsbury and on to Sherborne. Then in 1754, another was built from Askerswell to Bridport and on to Honiton in Devon. Through the rest of the century, especially during the era when George III was a regular resident, more toll roads were built and maintained throughout Dorset and Weymouth and its immediate neighbours had their very own turnpike trust. The trust leased out the rights to individuals to collect the tolls at the various toll booths built for that purpose, with the trusts taking a percentage of the profits and when necessary, they paid employees to help run the business.

In order to determine the cost of the toll, toll-house keepers had a complex pricing system they had to follow; they measured the width of the vehicle and its wheels and took in to account how many horses were pulling it. The narrower the wagon and the fewer the horses pulling it, the cheaper, because this meant less wear and tear on the road. Others had weigh engines and weigh bridges, which determined the weight of the vehicle and its load, meaning they charged by weight rather than width. There were some who were allowed to travel without paying, which included anyone who worked in animal husbandry, members of the military and anyone headed to church services. And of course, toll avoidance was always a problem, especially if there was a way to cross a waterway in order to bypass the toll house.

Weymouth's toll houses were located on what is today Radipole Spa Road, on the south side of the village; at Melcombe Narrows; the Backwater Bridge in Melcombe Regis; at Preston Road at the end of Melcombe Regis; and in Wyke Regis at Ferrybridge, the most profitable of all the tolls at £500 per year by the end of the 18th century, which explains why it was also the only toll booth in Dorset to have twenty-four-hour a day armed guards. By the 1880s, the trusts were dissolved and most toll roads were no longer charging anyway; the toll houses were either demolished or turned in to private homes, like the one in Charminster.

Millions of tonnes…the apes

Although Dorset's earliest permanent residents used stone to build, it was the Romans who began quarrying for commercial purposes. Industrial use of Portland stone, as well as the stone from other local sources like Preston, Portesham and Upwey, was important to the local economy for centuries; 15th century records indicate Preston stone was used in buildings as far away as London, as well as in local churches and homes during the building booms of the 13th and 15th centuries. There was also a small quarry in Wyke Regis, which was most likely the source for building Wyke's 15th century church. In the 17th century, architect Christopher Wren spent years coming and going from Portland as he designed and supervised the building of London's St. Paul's Cathedral and though his relationship with the quarrymen was often acrimonious at best, the cathedral was just one of the many buildings constructed of Portland stone in London during that time. Wren was insistent that the island's stone was the very best and he would except no other. It never lost its popularity after the success of that huge project.

In 1712, there were about 400 men and boys working in Portland's quarries; by 1770, Portland stone sold for 9d per cubic foot and that same year, 9,000 tonnes of stone shipped from the harbour. The industry owned 90 horses and employed 25 ships to haul the stone down the steep slopes of the Isle and to ship to ports around the country. By 1812, the quarrying business had doubled, with 800 men and boys, 180 horses and 50 ships working the Portland quarries. The men produced, hauled and loaded 25 thousand tonnes of saleable stone each year or roughly 30 tonnes per man. To do this, they had to shift 100 thousand tonnes of over burden, the useless excess – scree - in order to produce that saleable stone. Part of the reason for the increase was that with the Industrial Revolution came a lot of acidic smoke which blackened stone buildings in the areas most affected by the new industry. The exception was buildings built from Portland stone, which, because of its

> **Maggot and Sturt**
>
> Before the building of the breakwater began, a Royal Commission examined the Portland stone industry. They determined in 1839 that stone from the north eastern part of the island was better quality than that from the western part. At that point, many of the quarries were owned by the crown, but the commission's report said that the best were still privately held. Those included the Waycroft, Wide Street, Maggot, Fancy, Weston Independent, Inmosthay, Tout, Bowers, Grove, Under Kingbarrow, Goslings, Vern, Higher Down, Sturt, Yelland Cliffs, Withies Croft, Combe Fields and Portland Bill.

particular qualities, did not discolour the way other types of stone did. But it is the building of the breakwater that sees the island's ancient industry increase to produce huge amounts of stone, more than ever before.

One of the many challenging problems the quarrymen had was transporting the huge and incredibly heavy stones from the top of the island to the bottom, where it would then be loaded onto ships. For centuries, the quarries that ran along the edges of Portland's east side were able to use winches and cranes to get the stone to the piers for loading; by the end of the 18th century, those quarries were running out of viable stone and were moving further in to the centre of Portland. That meant transportation was far more difficult than ever before and the solution was to use even more of the traditional cross-land transport method employed for years: horses. An 1804 account of this process, written by a Somerset rector, Reverend J. Skinner, who visited the area that year, documents what a cruel process this part of quarrying really was:

Large hewn stones lie scattered in all directions, indeed the quarries worked on the Island are prodigious, and the mode of conveying the ponderous masses down the steep slopes unavoidably arrests the attention of the stranger: the blocks being placed on a strong wooden carriage, with solid wheels apportionate to the weight they are to sustain. Two horses are harnessed, on before and one (and sometimes two) behind, the latter being supplied with strong breeching in order to act as drawbacks to the carriage, and prevent its running with too great a velocity down the steep hills. Indeed, the sagacity and exertions of these poor animals in this arduous employment is really astonishing; they squat down on their haunches and suffer themselves to be dragged for many yards, struggling with all their strength against the weight that forces them forwards. To one unaccustomed to the sight, it appears as though their limbs must inevitably be dislocated, or their sinews cracked by the violence of their exertions. Indeed, one is compassionate to these poor creatures, the rather as all this labour might easily be obviated by the simple construction of a rail-road. Why this has not been long since performed is to me surprising, especially as Portland stone is in universal request.

The local name for these abused creatures was the Ape Horses, perhaps because of the strange contortions they had to go through in order not to be dragged to their deaths. The good Reverend was deeply moved, and disgusted, by what he witnessed and perhaps because of his compassion for what must have been other 19th century behaviours offensive to the sensitive, he committed suicide, but not until he had sketched the parts of Dorset he explored, to include some of East Dorset's barrows; one of those he actually dug himself, discovering Neolithic remains.

Reverend Skinner was a well-travelled and very educated man and he no doubt knew that by 1800, Britain had 1500 miles of industrial railway lines; the Surrey Iron Railway opened in 1803 and was the world's first public rail system and had been authorized by an act of Parliament. For whatever reason, though, the quarry owners chose to continue their cruel practices for another twenty years after Skinner's visit. That is until the growing demand for stone meant that a safer and better system of transport became a necessity rather than a luxury.

Operated by weighted pulleys

A group of quarry owners, London stone merchants and others with interests in the industry came together in 1824 in order to draw up plans for a railway dedicated to hauling stone. Once that had been done, they moved very quickly, especially motivated by the fact that as it turned out, the railroad was not going to be as expensive as they had thought, an assumption that had helped slow the move toward building one for years. As it turned out, a better transport system meant greater profits, not fewer, for the industry.

By the end of the year, plans were drawn up and the path of the rail was decided on: it was to be built along a ledge at the top of the island, running east toward Priory Corner, and on to the Verne's earthworks. From there, a steep incline would take it close to Portland Castle. This was to be operated by weighted pulleys, not horses, although horses were still going to be used to haul the wagons from quarry to rail line. The plan included making the railway a public company, requiring the organizers to seek parliamentary approval, which it did in June 1825.

Be of Public Utility

The preamble to the act making the Portland Railway Company public stated its aims: Whereas the making and maintaining of a railway or tramway for the passage of waggons and other carriages from certain lands called Priory Lands…to the stone piers near Portland Castle, on the northern coast of the said Island…and wold tend to the improvement of the estates… In the vicinity of the said railway or tramway, and in other respects be of public utility…

The Merchant's Railway

Within a few years of construction, the Portland Railway Company, more commonly referred to as the Merchants' Railroad, had a few growing pains; tracks, wagons, wheels, axles and other parts were damaged and land slippages along the route were a serious problem. These issues led to the company going in to debt, a problem that continued in to the 1830s and 40s. By 1844, the line was declared "deplorable," in spite of having hired a contractor to keep up the maintenance. Through the 1840s, there were ongoing problems with management of the line and by the 1850s, merchants were unhappy with the poor service; they simply could not get enough of the stone they required. Throughout that decade and into the next, the problems experienced by the company, its directors and its contractors – those men who were paid a certain amount per tonne of stone in guarantee of pickup and delivery and the maintenance and equipping of the line – struggled to maintain it; this had much to do with the lack of strong direction and business acumen, but either way, the Merchant's Railway never really ran smoothly during its first four decades.

In 1864, there were some minor but important changes made to parts of the line, which helped improve service, in turn helping to bring in more revenue to the company. The same year, a second line was built at the bottom of the line in order to make it much easier to get the stone to the loading piers. This again helped raise company revenues, with almost 71,000 tonnes of stone hauled that same year, bringing in almost £3,000 (£130,000 today) of revenue.

Weymouth's Own Railway

Not long after the Merchant's Railway was built, there were several schemes to bring a rail system into Weymouth from other parts of the country. The first idea was to build a line from Bath to Weymouth; that was proposed in 1836, but the idea was dropped because of a general lack of interest. In 1844, another was suggested, this one from Salisbury to Weymouth; the same year, the Bristol and Exeter Railway also proposed a branch to Weymouth, this one from Yeovil as part of their new line. Then, the Great Western Railway (GWR) created the Wilts, Somerset and Weymouth Railway (WSWR); the larger company hoped that by establishing a local company, it would attract local investment. The new rail company wanted to build a line from Chippenham to Weymouth via Yeovil and Dorchester. It received the go ahead when an Act of Parliament permitting it passed in June 1845. In spite of its popularity, the company experienced serious financial problems and had to be finished by GWR, which ended up spending over £1,400,000 (£6,200,000 today) to complete the line. Branch lines to Sherborne and Bridport had to be scrapped because of the lack of funds and even a link between the Weymouth station and a short line to the harbour were put on hold for years.

The Weymouth line finally opened in 1857 and though it had been the project of the GWR, the London and South Western Railroad (LSWR) had also gone ahead and created its own Weymouth connection, with a junction built between the two lines at Dorchester. This was just before the decision had been made to create a universal gauge, meaning railroads could not use other companies' tracks. The companies ran on different gauges and mixed gauge rails were laid into Weymouth, allowing both the GWR and the LSWR to reach the town. It travelled from Dorchester, paralleling the old Roman road, through Upwey, and into Melcombe Regis.

Brunel at the Station

The Weymouth Railway station was opened on the 20th of January, 1857, as the terminus of the Wiltshire, Somerset and Weymouth Railway (WS and WR) line from Chippenham. It was built on marshland reclaimed from the Wey River's backwater, rested on piles driven deep into the ground. The original station buildings were designed by an assistant of Isambard Kingdom Brunel, T. H. Bertram, who was responsible for quite a few of the rail buildings for the Great Western lines. It was constructed of wood, with a glazed roof spanning the tracks. The single-storey station housed offices, toilets and waiting rooms. There were two platforms with three roads between them; two were used for storage, with an engine release road between them. Unfortunately, as holiday traffic increased in the latter half of the nineteenth century, it was realized that those centre tracks should have had their own platforms. After the station was built, Brunel travelled to the new station to take a close look at his assistant's work.

Crowds of spectators...

Sadly, that grand opening of this long awaited station was not well publicized and the locals barely noticed that they finally had rail service. But Weymouth council called for a public holiday the following week and this second opening saw huge celebrations taking place a week later, the 27th of January; this time, locals came out in style, and, as stated by the Dorset County Chronicle, *a general holiday was observed by all classes*. St. Mary's and St. Thomas streets were decorated with flags and arches by the council and a military band marched through the high street. The GWR made 300 free tickets available, which were handed out when the crowds reached the station, where a beautiful locomotive and its cars had been prepared for the party. The revellers boarded and made it to Yeovil in only an hour, unheard of prior to this, when the trip would have taken all day by coach.

The Chronicle recorded that along the way the travellers *having been greeted at the various stations along the line by many sympathising demonstrations in the shape of colours displayed, the firing of cannon, and the shouts of crowds of spectators*. Later there was a lavish dinner and a ball held at the Royal and Victoria Hotels.

Tourism is back

In bringing rail service to Weymouth, the plan was to serve the growing number of working and middle class tourists who were using the new railroads being built around the country to travel cheaply to resorts and other places of interest; wherever the railroad went, towns prospered. Its other purpose was to offer secondary transport to travellers who arrived from the Channel Islands to Weymouth port via the local ferries, on the same line that had been ferrying locals and islanders back and forth since the late 18th century; the origins of that service go back to 1794 when the Post Office chose Weymouth as an official port to host a regular mail packet service to the Islands. The plan worked and after years of decline in tourism, the railway brought tourists back to Weymouth.

Steam packet

The railways were not the only thriving businesses based on the new-found interest in Portland harbour. It began with that appointment of Weymouth as an official port by the post office. It meant packet boats were in and out on a weekly basis, taking mainland mail and delivering it to the Channel Islands, which in turn led to improvements to harbour facilities. In 1827, the first innovative packet boats that were kept at Weymouth were the Ivanhoe and the Watersprite and these were steamers rather than the earlier sail boats. A year later, the steamer Meteor was added to the tiny fleet, but it was wrecked at Church Ope Cove two years later. By the late 1830s, the post office handed over responsibility for the mail service from Weymouth to the admiralty and in 1839, the Commercial Steam Packet Company which operated a paddle steamer service from London to Weymouth began to offer twice weekly trips to and from Cherbourg, so for the first time, Weymouth residents and those from neighbouring communities could travel from their own harbour to France.

Meanwhile, as the railroad service that would eventually reach Weymouth was expanding from London to Southampton, a group of businessmen, one a local innkeeper called George Peace Scott, got together to create the Weymouth and Southampton Steam Packet Company and theirs was the first of its kind to actually be registered in Weymouth. The plan was to take local passengers from Weymouth to Southampton, where they would then travel by rail to London. Though there was an efficient overland coach system from Weymouth to Southampton called the Emerald, the idea was to offer a slightly faster and much less bone shattering trip, which was more interesting, because it was by sea. Passengers could also carry much more luggage or other goods on the ship than they could via coach. The plan was quite brave, as the Commercial Steam Packet Company was already running two different routes, the London to Cherbourg via Weymouth and the London,

Southampton, Weymouth, Torquay and Dartmouth. But these were twice weekly and the Weymouth and Southampton Steam Packet Company wanted to offer daily services. This inevitably led to competition between the two packet companies, with the Commercial Steam Packet Company adding more routes and the competing Weymouth Company trying to raise a lot of money to add more ships to their single ship, the Rose. This did not happen, however, as the company continued to provide important services, but was faced with yet more outside competition. The admiralty also decided to take away Weymouth's status as the provider of post packets to the Channel Islands in 1845, transferring it to Southampton.

But all was not lost to the Rose and her owners; a local brewer who was also a company director, garnered the support of some Dorset farmers and cattle dealers, who were happy to use the company's services to ship their goods, moving the focus of the local company to the movement of goods rather than people, though it continued to offer regular services as well as leisure excursions. Even that, however, could not save the Rose and her owners and she was sold off. Competition was just too intense for this early innovator to survive.

Then along came the Cosens family.

> **The Rose**
>
> This small steamer was a popular site in Weymouth and was ahead of her time, with refreshments available on board, just as modern ferries offer today, as well as women stewards, a job described at the time as someone who attended passengers on conveyance. Women servers on "conveyances" in the mid-19th century was very unusual, but at sea, unheard of.

Cosens of Weymouth

A Lyme Regis family, the husband a seafarer, moved to Weymouth with two sons, and another was born in Weymouth, in the late 1810s. The Cosens' eldest son, Joseph, who became a sailor, was very familiar with Weymouth and Southampton Steam Packet Company's boom and then bust and he would also have been witness to the huge projects going on around him with the building of Portland Harbour's breakwater. He saw an opportunity to offer an alternative to the only way to get from Portland to Weymouth and back, by providing a steamer service to those who wanted a faster route than going across the narrow causeway by foot, horse or carriage. Cosens of Weymouth's service began in 1848, with four sailings a day and like the Rose, it offered not just passenger service, but the shipment of goods to and from. Business boomed and with the building of the Verne and all the prisoners who had to be transported to Portland, Cosens did very well. Joseph also re-established services to the Channel Islands and offered a variety of private sailings and tourist excursions, to include those that gave visiting tourists a chance to view all the building going on in and around the harbour.

Like earlier steamer companies, it did not take long for Cosens to attract rivals for the Weymouth to Portland trade, when a meeting was called at a Fortuneswell pub to attract local investors to another possible company offering the same or similar services; this was only three years after Cosens had begun to trade. These new rivals, made up of a group of local businessmen who invested in the new company, called the new venture the Weymouth and Portland Steam Packet Company. Interestingly, some of the investors also became involved in the Weymouth rail projects which were related, directly and indirectly, to the breakwater construction. This was seen by some as a conflict of interest, as the railroad coming to Weymouth and Portland was in direct competition, some thought, with steamer services.

As could be expected, the rival steamer companies did not always get along; they argued over rights of landing and like-issues, but were a vital part of travel to and from Weymouth, as well as providing help with towing and raising ships that were victims of rough seas and the difficult passage along Chesil and around Portland. Steamers could manoeuvre in challenging situations in a way that sailing ships could not. As the 19th century went on, Cosen's then invested in tug boats, which became an important part of the lucrative Cosen's shipping empire, as they were part of many salvage attempts. By the turn of the 20th century, in spite of all the competition, the company was still going strong, with its own foundry, engineering works and foundry cottages which housed some of its workers. It did not cease service until the 1960s.

A bridge across Radipole

Immediately after the railroad came to Weymouth, various companies and individuals began pushing for a line from Weymouth to Portland, both for the transport of goods and people. The first proposal was made in 1857, the same year the Weymouth line was opened, but there was little support for it and it was dropped. Two more proposals were made in 1861, one from a local consortium of businessmen, and eventually both groups joined forces at a meeting that same year; they began by figuring out the best route. There were some who were not happy about the idea of a Weymouth and Portland line because they feared it would encourage a full-service port at Portland, offering the same services Weymouth's offered. But that opposition was dropped and the Weymouth and Portland Railway Act of Parliament, a process required in order to get permission to build tracks on public and crown land, received the Royal Assent in June 1862. The rail companies bought enough land to allow for the track to expand, if necessary, in later years. Construction started in December 1862 with the intention of completing the line by January 1864. The contractor chosen was John Aird and Company, one of the leading British civil engineering businesses of the time, which was based in London. It was the same company that had been hired to move Crystal Palace in 1851.

By early October 1863, construction was progressing well; huge pilings were driven into Radipole Lake, with the Backwater viaduct running up along the rise above Weymouth, through Rodwell, and into Wyke Regis. A second viaduct over the Fleet at Ferrybridge was also well on to its way to completion. The only other major engineering features - a cut-and-cover tunnel taking the line under Wyke Road at Rodwell and the 700-foot long Marsh embankment which took the line over a former inlet of the harbour - were also progressing well. The Marsh embankment was completed by the end of February 1864 and the first train to travel over the entire length of the line ran in May.

The project hit its first problem when the Board of Trade carried out its initial inspection in May 1864. Their report rated the two viaducts as *very unsatisfactory*, was critical of the signalling arrangements at Portland Junction in Weymouth, and listed a number of other points that required serious improvements. Until the problems were solved, the rail line could not be opened. It was inspected again in August 1864, but there were still issues that had not been remedied. The problem turned out to be a complete lack of agreement between the three organizations involved in the building: The Great Western Railway, the London and South Western Railway and the local company carrying out the management of the works, the Weymouth and Portland Board. The latter thought that it should not have to supply a separate station on the line, but the London group wanted one and wanted the Weymouth group to pay for it. And the arguments went on.

Coming to no agreement, the line sat unused for over a year. Eventually, with no agreement in site, the three groups took it to arbitration and it was ruled that the Weymouth and Portland Board had to pay Great Western almost £3000 for land and improvements to the junction between the branch and the main line, something that had to be done in order to pass the necessary inspection. In spite of the ruling, there was still no agreement over the particulars and this impacted the Weymouth Quay tramway, which was ready to open, but could not begin its service because it was part of the stalled railroad system. Finally, in 1865, the groups agreed to a plan and the Board of Trade gave its permission to open the line. Goods were loaded and carried for the first time on the 16th of October that year, followed by passenger service a week later. Sadly, once the companies finally had the line up and running, they were overly ambitious and offered far too many trains and found they had to cut back on their initial services. After all the problems the railroad had been through, the public did not rush to use the line.

The Admiralty Line

As the breakwater and its related projects first began, the quarrymen supplying the stone for the project used a gravity-operated rail system – dubbed the Admiralty Line - that began construction in 1848 to transport the stone from the top of the island to the bottom. The two systems, the Merchant's and the Admiralty lines, worked in conjunction with one another, though the latter was funded by the government, not a private company; the Admiralty ran from the Grove to the east side of the Verne, and on to the corner of the island where the building of the breakwater began. In 1849, more quarrying started at the Verne, where the stone was removed in order to create the "moat" around what would be the huge fort. That stone was lowered down the east side of the Verne by a rope-operated pulley system to meet up with the same system running down the island from the Grove. The incline at the Verne was very steep and required a huge overhead brake drum fitted with a screw brake controlling the cable for each of the three sections that made up the incline.

The loaded wagons descended and were unloaded after being weighed at the weighbridge, where the attendant also kept record of how many wagons passed through each day. The empty wagons were then hauled back up the hill on two separate rail tracks. As the stone was hauled and placed on the staging built of huge pilings along the line that was to become the breakwater, railway tracks, five abreast, were laid along the wall. These had to handle wagons each loaded with ten tonnes of stone rolling along the track while being pounded by the sea. These were pushed into place at each point the stone had to be unloaded; a pin in the wagon was removed, and the back of the wagon dropped allowing the weight of the stone to propel the whole load out of the wagon. As more and more stone was laid, more track followed.

After the project reached the point that the base for the circular section of the Breakwater Fort had to be built, the Admiralty trains delivered loads of stone to a very specialized piece of equipment. This *mechanical traveller*, a unique crane, worked by lifting the loaded wagons up and spilling out their contents in a semi-circle. The *traveller* was steam operated and made spreading so much heavy stone in a circular pattern much easier than if it had been done by men moving each stone, piece by piece. *Travellers* were also used to shift huge stones that were fitted by men working on the staging, directing the delivery of the stones to their places, working in conjunction with the mariner masons who were underwater making sure the stones were fitting properly under the waterline.

The Admiralty railroad had its share of accidents; in 1853, the first big disaster happened when the staging of a part of the breakwater collapsed. A locomotive, eight workers and four wagons fell into the sea. The locomotive and wagons were eventually recovered, but two workmen were drowned. And there were other deadly accidents, to include one that demonstrated the strange draw the breakwater, railways and quarries had for locals and visitors alike. There was a walkway running along the breakwater construction staging, intended to encourage people to take an interest in the massive project; a woman who was site seeing got her long skirt caught in the wheel of a stone wagon passing along and she was dragged under and killed by the heavy vehicle. Other fatalities often involved failed brakes and problems with the pulley systems controlling the steep inclines the wagons had to traverse. Men were either crushed when they fell off of a runaway wagon, or died on impact at the bottom of the incline.

Additional Powers Act of 1871

There had been talk of creating connections between the three railroad systems; during the early construction of the breakwater, there was a basic line run from the Admiralty line to the Merchant's, where they met in Castletown, but there was no direct connection between those two or the Weymouth line. Then in September 1870, the Dorset County Chronicle ran an article about future plans to create just that: *The works for the extension of the Weymouth and Portland Railway to the Breakwater will commence on October 1st*. This was either incorrect insider information or simply guess work, as it was another year later that the parties involved came to an agreement to build such a connection. It was recorded in the Great Western Railway Additional Powers Act of 1871, which allowed for a mile-long track between the Weymouth and Admiralty lines.

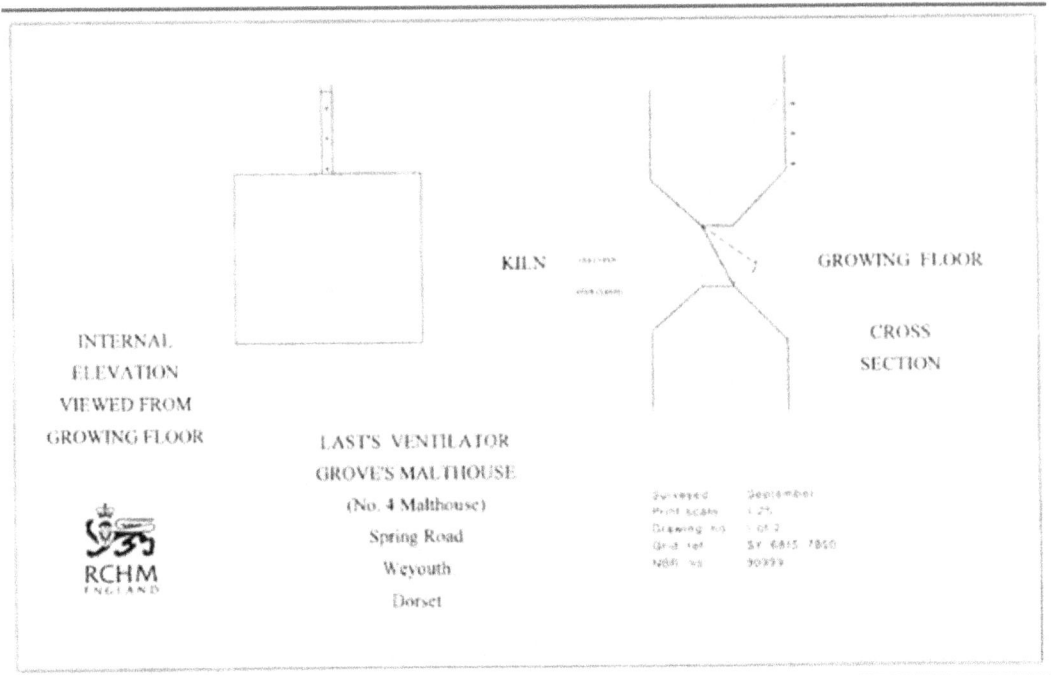

INTERNAL
ELEVATION
VIEWED FROM
GROWING FLOOR

KILN

GROWING FLOOR

CROSS
SECTION

LAST'S VENTILATOR
GROVE'S MALTHOUSE
(No. 4 Malthouse)
Spring Road
Weymouth
Dorset

RCHM
ENGLAND

Food and Drink

This has been, time immemorial, a Dairy District. The Rural Economy of the West of England, 1796

By the end of the 18th century, Dorset farmers had enjoyed increased sales because of the excellent road that had been built from Weymouth to Bridport; those farmers who specialized in butter and mutton, for instance, had easy access to that road and were able to communicate with the two important towns and their local villages in order to keep up with what was selling and which ships were available for the transporting of goods that were produced for export.

As early as the mid-1700s, the quality of Dorset butter was recorded by visitors from London and with ever-increasing road access, by the 1840s, its butter was said to hold *the highest rank* and as *pleasant to the taste and preferred by many to the richer qualities of other districts.* Conversely, local cheeses were not as widely appreciated. In mid-century, a visitor described Dorset *skim cheese* as *more fitted to be used as barrow-wheels than for food.*

When the railroad came to Dorset, that helped even more, as Weymouth, Portland, Bridport, Dorchester and Poole had main lines that allowed the farms running between them to take advantage of this new and faster form of shipping and helped to increase their potential markets. Significant disparities between those areas of the county with rail service and those in the central uplands without grew to be a problem, a bigger one than any other county in England, helping fuel an agrarian crisis which changed the face of Dorset farming forever. But, it also increased dairy farming, which led to further specialization, which in turn meant quite a shift in population and a strong agricultural economy. Weymouth and its neighbours maintained and increased old dairies like those in Broadwey, Sutton Poyntz, Ringstead and Wyke Regis and others were built or improved upon, to include Bincombe, East Fleet, Bagwell and Osmington. These areas stopped growing large cereal crops in favour of the more profitable dairy farming, and that left this much less profitable farming to those areas of Dorset without close rail service, which meant a shift in population and poverty for those farmers, versus relative prosperity for those who worked in the dairy industry. Labourers who moved with the trend maintained their lifestyles, those who could not, experienced hardships similar to earlier in the century, after the Napoleonic Wars.

The century of ale

Although there were many poor crop years leading up to the middle of the 19th century, there were other Dorset farmers who thrived because of the ever-increasing demand for beer, which meant those whose land produced high yields of wheat and barley did very well for themselves. Beer had been, for thousands of years, brewed by housewives for family consumption, but as more and more inns were built from the Middle Ages on, those facilities brewed their own, marking the beginning of professional brewing. Even the housewives who continued to home brew used the growing number of village malt houses that were appearing in villages like Abbotsbury by the 17th century, as did many of the inns, as malt had become an important "modern" ingredient in beer brewing and malting was not done at home. Many Dorset villages also had their own grain mills; Portland had mills across the island as did many towns and villages throughout Dorset.

Villages and towns like Chickerell, Wyke Regis, Fontwell Magna, Blandford, Abbotsbury, Melcombe Regis, Bridport, Lyme Regis, Lychett Matravers, Cerne Abbas, Portland and many others had their own breweries by or before the 19th century, some of them attached to public houses, others independents selling to those houses and inns.

Maltsters

The tiny village of Cerne Abbas was not so tiny in past centuries; before the Dissolution, it was a thriving Church community, but after that, its success was due more to its industry, especially beer. In 1705, Cerne came into the ownership of the Pitt family of Stratfield Saye in Hampshire and it flourished as a small market town with a population of 1500. Its underground water, according to a Bishop Pococke, made the village *more famous for beer than in any other place in the kingdom.* Cerne beer was even exported to North

America, but plenty of it was consumed much closer; by 1747 the village had seventeen public inns and taverns. In the 1798 survey of the village, Thomas Coombs was listed as a *Maltster, Brewer and Linen Draper*, along with six other *Maltsters*, more evidence that Cerne was a very important brewing community indeed.

Chapelhay water and Radipole barley

Going back to at least the 13th century, Weymouth was one of the communities in Dorset with an established tradition of professional beer brewing. Although the River Wey would have been a convenient water source, its frequent use as an open sewer and the fact that the water itself was brackish meant that the water for brewing had to come from the natural springs all around the community and its surrounding villages. Many of the springs were tapped into via wells, which provided the majority of the drinking water consumed in the area for millennia. The spring water was delicious because it filtered naturally through the local limestone. This was probably why the local Celts, who actually began the local tradition of brewing beer, were able to produce so much of it. The tradition continued through the Roman era, although they introduced wine to the British diet. After the Romans left, the tradition was revived in a big way and Weymouth certainly led the way in the return of the Celtic tradition.

The main brewery of Weymouth was established on what is today Brewer's Quay and there had been a brewery operating there from at least the mid-13th century up to the 1980s. It was the perfect site for a brewery because of the spring at Chapelhay and because the farmers of Radipole grew the barley needed for a good brew. In 1742, this brewery was owned by the Flew family and it was in the 18th century when Dorset saw a really dynamic brewing industry arise, one that enriched a number of owners; most of the beer consumed, for instance, by shipwrights and sailors at the Royal Dockyards during the 19th century was brewed in Dorset. Another family called Devenish took over the business in the 1820s. This family had a centuries' long relationship with brewing; one of their forebears had been appointed supervisor of all British brewers by King Edward IV in 1462. The Devenish family continued to brew in Weymouth until the 1980s.

Mr. Pigot's directory

In 1842, shortly after the first national census but before the harbour was built, the total population of Weymouth, to include Melcombe Regis, was about 7,750. In this small town there were, according to the local directory of *Mr. J. Pigot*, no less than 51 outlets selling beer, which meant that there were 152 persons per outlet. According to a study by Cambridge University in 1995, the national average at the time for such outlets was about 186 per head of the population. Out of the 51, 27 were pubs and inns and the other 24 were small brewers who retailed their beer for home and work consumption, often offering free delivery of their product. Some even offered customers the brewer family's parlour to enjoy their pint if they preferred. It is possible that the reason for so many brewers was because of the Weymouth and Portland ports; sailors liked their rum, but beer was also a favourite. And of course, water was not considered safe to drink, beer was. After the railway was completed, Portland pubs and inns were also able to bring the necessary hops to the Isle to brew their own and to "import" beer from Weymouth brewers. There were also many new pubs established there, responding to the increasing demand of Portland's own growing population.

By 1898, with the completion of the harbour in 1872 and all that meant to the community, and with the arrival of large numbers of naval personnel, the picture changes considerably. The population had risen to approximately 14,500 and only 15 small independent beer sellers were left, as listed in another directory, Kelly's, that year, compared to 73 licensed pubs and inns, which meant there was one outlet to every 165 people. There had been a considerable shift of emphasis on drinking habits at this point, going from private to public consumption, probably more so because of the large military presence. The loss of the independents could also in part have been due to the continued improvements in water supply, as well as the fact that tea had become much cheaper by the end of the 19th century. The development of the temperance movement would likely also have had an impact.

Another Weymouth brewer was John Groves. Groves was a respected businessman and owner of John Groves & Sons, Ltd., Hope Brewery, also located in Weymouth's quay. He served as the town mayor three times, from 1886 to 1889, and he was also a poor house guardian for his Rodwell parish, well known for his kindness to the poor, especially for the baskets of coal he gave out to poor families at Christmas.

This brewer was also known in the community for the beautiful building he erected in memory of his son, Sidney Groves, who died very young of pleurisy. The "Sidney Grove Memorial Hall" was intended for use by local civic and youth groups, to include the Church Lads Brigade, which Sidney had been a member of. Its official opening was officiated by Lord Chelmsford, General Frederic Thesiger, best known for his military service during the Crimean and Anglo-Zulu Wars. Over the years, many branches of the military used the building and it served as a military hospital during WWI for the wounded being brought to Weymouth from the French trenches, and later as the National School after the school's original building was bombed during WWII.

The Abstainers

The English temperance movement began in Preston, Lancashire, when seven men signed a pledge in 1832, declaring they would not touch another drop of alcohol. The leader of this fledging movement was a working class merchant and social activist. He also had a great gift for public speaking and publicity and it was his efforts that pushed this tiny movement south, where it spread to become a national campaign, helped by the churches across the country; the Church of England had its own Temperance Society and the Methodists pushed the anti-drinking message by building temperance halls in order to provide "alternative" social activities that did not involve drinking. More and more, throughout the 19th century, drink was demonised as the slippery slope, where working men drank their wages away, leaving families destitute. Authors like Dorset's Thomas Hardy included this theme in a number of his books, like Jude the Obscure, which is set on Portland and demonises alcohol and with his character Henchard in the Mayor of Casterbridge who struggles with drink. Hardy himself was involved in the local temperance movement and his anti-drinking message is found in much of his writing.

Even the army got involved. By the middle of the 19th century, each regiment had its own Temperance Association and they implemented special medals which were awarded to soldiers who stayed away from drink for allotted amounts of time. A Dorset newspaper helps tell the story of the military's efforts to stop drinking in the ranks:

THE DORSET MILITIA AT WEYMOUTH

During the month the "boys of Dorset" have been undergoing their annual training on the Nothe. Various efforts have been made to promote the cause of temperance, or rather total abstinence from strong drink, in the ranks, and with this object in view numbers of the men have been invited to social gatherings, which have been of an interesting and beneficial character. The largest of the kind was that on Monday evening at the Holy Trinity Infant School room, where the local committee of the Church of England Temperance Association provided tea for two hundred men, and afterwards gave them a pleasant entertainment consisting of singing, music, conjuring, and speeches. Mr. and Mrs. Crabb of the "Three Cups" Coffee Tavern, were entrusted with the sole responsibility of providing the tea, and they fulfilled it right well. The School room was completely crammed, yet the wants of all were well attended to and the catering gave the utmost satisfaction. After tea the entertainment, which was of a most successful character, took place, several ladies and gentlemen kindly volunteering their services. Amongst these may be mentioned in the musical line the Rev. W.S. and Mrs, Shuttleworth, Miss Addison, Miss Dancey, Mrs. Hixon, Miss Dowding, Miss East, the Rev. R.C. Gilbert, and Major Gollop. Mr. R.G. Wilson created much amusement with his sleight of hand tricks, and subsequently appeared amongst the speakers, among whom were the Rev. J.D. Addison, Rev. J. Stephenson, and Rev. H. Pelham Stokes of Wareham. After tea the song "Britons shall never be Slaves" was sung, the men joining most heartily in the chorus, this being followed by "Home Sweet Home," sung by Mrs.

Hixon, the Militia taking up the chorus. After a few remarks from the Rev. J. Eddison, Miss Dancey sang "Summer Showers," which was encored, and the Rev. W.S. Shuttleworth gave "My Polly." The Rev H. Pelham Stokes said he considered it to be a great honour to speak a few words on behalf of the cause which was so dear to the noblest in the land, and they ought to be thankful and rejoice that the army coffee tavern movement was so dear to the heart of the Commander in Chief, the Duke of Cambridge, as also H.R.H. the Duke of Connaught, who was every inch a soldier. They all know some of their finest soldiers became victims of drink, and to whatever sin they yielded they were sure to be a slave to it. The second of June, 1881.

By 1889, Weymouth had three temperance hotels along the seafront and by 1898, that number had gone up to seven. Other Dorset communities also had their own dedicated anti-alcohol hotels, to include Dorchester, Wimborne (a temperance boarding house), Fortune's Well (old spelling), Milborne, Blandford, Gillingham, to name just some of them. Broadwey, Gillingham, Poole, Portesham and Portland had their own temperance halls; Bridport appears to be the first to have established its own temperance "style" by opening the Bridport Coffee Tavern in 1879. The temperance movement also helped revive the concept of the coffee house, which had become popular in the 17th century; the early houses were all about having a place to meet to discuss politics, but this new approach was simply a way to allow men to get together, but remain sober.

Taxes and wharfingers…

Going all the way back to the Neolithic era, the local Celts, the Durotriges, travelled in and out of Weymouth harbour as they traded with other tribes living along the Dorset coast, as well as other tribal people as far away as Ireland, Spain and Italy. The Romans too saw the importance of both Portland's and Weymouth's harbours; they also traded from Dorset to places around their empire, to include the huge quantities of wine they brought in from today's France and Italy. Then beginning in the 7th century, the Saxons arrived and they too were great traders and made full use of the local harbours.

In 1817, Weymouth became a bonding port by order of the Lords of the Privy Council; this meant the town was required to maintain a warehouse for the purpose of holding dutiable goods until the duty was paid by the importer. Those goods included alcohol and tobacco and the order of council was an indication of the continued importance of the port, in spite of its loss of shipping over the years, mostly due to the silting up of the harbour. Weymouth was also one of the few English ports that employed *wharfingers*; this was a man or men who acted as wharf managers, whose jobs included day-to-day duties like keeping the slipways clear and tidy, keeping the tide tables and, importantly, resolving disputes amongst the users of the port; sailors, captains and ships' owners were not always known for their diplomatic abilities. Wharfingers would also have been responsible for helping with the duties' warehouse. In a local directory of 1844, two of these *wharfingers* were listed; they were a Mr. Beales and a Mr. Cox.

Long before the railroad arrived in Weymouth, the harbour had ceased to be the busy commercial port it had once been, but there were still traces of that earlier method of transporting goods. Cargo continued to arrive from the Mediterranean, as well as North America; coal was imported from Northern England as well as Wales, and timber, brandy, tobacco, rice, wine and gin came from various countries and other British ports. Wool, which had been a mainstay of the economy for at least 700 years, was still being produced throughout Dorset, to include around Weymouth and on Portland, with much of it ending up in Europe, where it had been valued for those many centuries.

Avoiding taxes...

When the first formal tax on the British people was imposed by Edward I in 1275, this changed the way some did business, especially those who traditionally used the harbours to land their trade goods: smuggling was born out of a desire to avoid paying tax and none in Britain were as good at this form of "trade" than Dorset locals. A huge percentage of Weymouth and its neighbours' residents had a role in smuggling. Wine and brandy were two of the favourite smuggled items, followed by other luxury products.

Smugglers found the eccentric coast an easy place to store and transport their goods, as they could stash them in the nooks and crannies of quarries, small bays and along the rugged coastal paths. They even devised clever ways to float large barrels of brandy in order to assure customs officials could not find their ill-gotten goods. They devised something they called "sewing the crop" where they weighted the barrels, floating them near a point of assignation, and when it was safe to do so, pull the barrels to shore. Then they often transferred the alcohol into much smaller casks, especially designed and made by local coopers; these were oddly shaped and designed to be carried by a man – or woman – either on foot or horseback. The long Chesil beach was a mecca for smugglers and the Fleet was especially popular; they found it a handy place to float their casks. Although monarch after monarch tried to stop smuggling, so many locals were involved, it was almost impossible to prevent it completely.

The 19th century efforts to stop the smuggling trade, however, were becoming more effective as the years went by, but local records indicate that many were still involved. They also demonstrate that quite a few smugglers or those suspected of smuggling ended up in the Dorchester gaol after being caught by custom's officers. From 1782 to 1853, smuggling and committing bodily harm to customs officials were two of the primary offences for which locals and others ended up in gaol. Seemingly tiny villages produced a lot of smugglers: from 1817 to 1841, eleven Abbotsbury residents were jailed. Those who were simply convicted of smuggling usually got off with a fine, but those who were found guilty of *assaulting and obstructing customs officers* were sent off to do hard labour.

Bridport was slightly unusual in that its smugglers, those who were gaoled between 1817 to 1842, were involved in the sailcloth and like-industries, rather than being sailors and fishermen and three of them were women; all of the women were arrested for assaulting customs officers. Tiny Burton Bradstock, one of the true haunts of smuggling for centuries, saw nine fishermen arrested for smuggling, most of them in 1836, half of them for violence against customs officers and one for 'making a light and fire as a signal to vessel.' Smugglers from Chickerell, eight of them, were arrested between 1816 and 1843 and one of them, Maria Bagwell, was a 23-year-old dressmaker. Five labourers from Portesham were gaoled between 1816 and 1835, seven from Preston from 1827 to 1843; Radipole had two arrests in 1833 and in 1843 and Sutton Poyntz saw six residents gaoled between 1791 and 1840.

Then there was Weymouth with 51 smugglers caught between 1809 and 1844. Most of them were labourers and seamen, but eight were women, most widows, probably struggling to earn enough money to feed themselves and their children. Perhaps the most interesting of those women was Martha Lumb who was sentenced to a harsh six-months hard labour for her smuggling. Two Wyke Regis seamen were caught along with the ferryman who operated the ferry at Smallmouth Bay, but the biggest supplier of local smugglers was Portland, with 106 gaoled between 1817 and 1845; most of the men were quarrymen and fishermen, but the twenty-one women who were arrested were an assortment of *fish women, carriers of fish*, and fish sellers, along with a shirt maker, needlewoman and a grocer. The only town or village that seems to have evaded the law was Melcombe Regis, with only one arrest during that time.

Others caught on the Dorset coast for smuggling between 1800 to 1843 were not locals and indicate just how big an "industry" it was during those years; there were dozens of Frenchmen gaoled locally, along with an assortment of mostly-seamen from the Isle of Wight, Pembroke, Guernsey, Jersey, Devon, Kent, Hampshire and Somerset. The French presence is not surprising given the ease with which they could sail the ancient route between Cherbourg and Weymouth, where French wine and brandy were still in such demand.

Lighting the way...

There have been attempts to make coastal Dorset safe for ships travelling at night going back to at least the Romans, but the official coastal lights were in the hill top chapels of Abbotsbury and St. Aldhelm's Head, where during the late middle ages, rushes and even candles burned every night in an attempt to help sailors navigate. The construction of a modern system of lighthouses around the British coast did not begin, however, until the 17th century (in East Anglia), spreading quickly as canny businessmen saw the potential for profit in building and maintaining them at public expense. The Trinity House Corporation, which was responsible for deciding where lighthouses would be placed, did not feel a lighthouse was necessary in the Weymouth area when a Cornwall speculator, Sir John Coryton, applied for permission in 1664 to build the first lighthouse at Portland Bill. It seems, however, their refusal was more about politics than an honest belief that there was no need to have a lighthouse on the Bill. It was and still is one of the most dangerous places to navigate in the UK, with five different currents meeting and where many ships over the centuries have met their ends.

A second try also failed, when Captain William Holman of Weymouth, supported by local ship owners and the Corporation of Weymouth, petitioned Trinity House again, only to be told there was no reason to build an expensive lighthouse on the Bill. Finally, in

1716, another petition on behalf of the people of Weymouth was accepted and King George I gave permission for the first lighthouse on the Dorset coast, with a sixty-one-year lease to a private consortium to build it. But the building was not well-maintained and the fires that acted as the light source often went unlit, proved by a 1752 inspection by Trinity House officials who reported *it was nigh two hours after sunset before any light appeared in either of the lighthouses.*

Finally, in 1789, William Johns, a Weymouth builder under contract to Trinity House, took down one of the towers at the Bill and erected a new one at a cost of £2,000 (£170,000 today); this was lit with six large Argand oil lamps rather than an open fire, the first lighthouse in Britain to have this kind of lighting. These were also fitted with lenses to increase the reflection. The light was designed and patented in France and ran on vegetable or whale oil. The lighthouse itself had been re-sited to assure that ships could see just where they needed to navigate to avoid the rough currents and the rocky out crops in order to make it through to the Channel or into Portland Roads. In 1798, the lighthouse was fitted with two cannons to protect it against Napoleon's threats of invasion.

In 1844, a seven-metre-tall white stone obelisk was built at the tip of Portland Bill as a warning of a low shelf of rock extending thirty metres into the sea; the obelisk still stands near the most recently built lighthouse, which was erected in 1906. Another two lighthouses were added in 1869.

In 1851, Portland's first breakwater light was built to help ships navigate that part of the harbour, as the building of the breakwater had actually added to the hazards of shipping along Portland and Weymouth's waters; in 1859, a lightship was placed on Shambles Shoal and other shore lights included one placed in 1867 on Weymouth's north pier and another on the south pier in 1896.

Shipwrecks and Wreckers...

And once on the beach, the sea has little mercy, for the water is deep right in, and the waves curl over full on the pebbles with a weight no timbers can withstand. Then if the poor fellows try to save themselves, there is a deadly undertow or rush-back of the water, which sucks them off their legs, and carries them again under the thundering waves. It is that back-suck of the pebbles that you may hear for miles inland, even at Dorchester, on still nights long after the winds that caused it have sunk, and which makes people turn in their beds, and thank God they are not fighting with the sea on Moonfleet Beach.

John Meade Faulkner, From *Moonfleet* 1898

The nature of the rocky, uneven coastline of Dorset has made it a dangerous place for the ships travelling along its shore for hundreds, probably thousands, of years, with or without lighthouses. There may have been as many as a thousand shipwrecks over those years and Weymouth and its neighbours saw their fair share, which is why the coastal area along Chesil Beach earned the nickname *Deadman's Bay*.

Although it actually went down near Poole, the San Salvador, a Spanish ship captured at Portland Bill when the Armada and the English navy met in battle during the Anglo-Spanish War there in 1588, is sometimes mentioned as the earliest recorded Dorset shipwreck. Given its new sails had not been fitted when it was being moved to Poole, this is unlikely be a valid claim, especially as most shipwrecks were caused by bad weather, which was not the case with the San Salvador. But what this first wreck has in common with so many others is the fact that somehow, mysteriously, some of the valuables which were supposed to go to the town of Weymouth and others to London mysteriously disappeared, probably taken by a combination of local officials and their compatriots, many of whom were "wreckers," those men and women who like their fellows, the smugglers, were very active along the coast; they were usually the first at the scene of a wreck and often used violent means to remove anything of value from struggling ships.

Twenty-two years later, it was reported that at least twenty ships were wrecked on Dorset shores during a fierce storm on Christmas day, 1600. Other shipwrecks closest to Weymouth and its neighbours include a Spanish ship that went down off of Burton Bradstock in 1629; this was looted by the locals before the king's officers arrived. Then there was a Dutch ship called the Golden Grape, which was also looted, but by both locals and its own crew. Wrecked near Wyke, there were hundreds of people watching it meet its fate, proving what an incredible system of communication local wreckers and their helpers maintained. The ship's gold found its way into the hands of people along the local coastline.

Seven of the crew were lost in the shipwreck, others were helped by a Wyke Regis innkeeper, who though he showed them great kindness, also helped himself to the gold some of those sailors had managed to remove from the ship.

In the 18th century, at least thirteen ships were wrecked and looting and fights between the looters and the customs officers were often a part of the process. When the Spanish ship the Jesus Maria Joseph wrecked on Chesil Beach in 1716, the customs officers tried to reach it to salvage anything they could, but they could not recover any of the cargo of wine. Their report described what the wreckers did to the officers; they were *Beat, Hounded and Resisted by the Countrie people*, a common reference to the locals, especially Portlanders. A year later, a French ship met the same fate at Chesil Cove and the customs officers were once again besieged by local wreckers: *Great numbers of Portland men came down upon us with Axes, Hatchetts, Clubbs, and beat us from the Good wounding Serverall of Us very much.* Although the Act of 1753 made wrecking a capital offence and called for transportation of those found to be *looting of wrecked vessels and their cargoes*, there was little the authorities could do but show up and attempt to control the situation, which they rarely did.

Though there were many other wrecks, most looted for the goods they carried, possibly the most spectacular was the multiple wreck of a small flotilla in 1795; the story of the Aeolus, Golden Grove, Thomas, Piedmont, Venus and Catherine as they crashed into Chesil Beach is a stark history of just how determined, and harsh, local wreckers could be, as described by one of the survivors as she wrote about one of the victims of the disaster:

While he lay in this situation, trying to recover breath and strength a great many people from the neighbouring villages passed him - they had crossed the Fleet water in the hopes of sharing what the lower inhabitants of this coast are too much accustomed to consider as their right, the plunder of the ships wrecked on their shore and, in the gratification of their avarice, they are too apt to forget humanity. Scenes like these call forth the most honourable, and discover the most degrading qualities of the human heart. Mr. Darley seems to have been so far from meeting with immediate assistance among here who were plundering the dead, without thinking of the living, (otherwise than to make some advantage of them also) that though he saw many boats passing and repassing the fleet water, he found great difficulty in procuring a passage over for himself and two or three of his fellow sufferers, who had by this time joined him: having, however, at length passed it, he soon met with Mr Bryer, Surgeon of Weymouth, to whose active humanity all the unhappy sufferers were greatly indebted; on his reaching Weymouth, the gentlemen of the South Gloucester sent him every supply of necessaries that his situation required - and all the soldiers and sailors were taken care of by Mr. Warne, Agent to the Commissioners for the Sick and Hurt.

From **The Loss of the Catharine, Venus, Piedmont, Thomas, Golden Grove and Ælous, 1795, on the Chesil Beach**

The 19th century saw its own share of shipwrecks along the Dorset coast. One of the first was a large ship especially built in Aberdeen for the valuable trade between Britain and the Far East; the Earl of Abergavenny was on its way from London to India in February, 1805. Also an East Indiaman, its final English port of call was Portsmouth. When it sailed, it had 402 passengers, which included men, women and children and a contingent of East India troops. The Abergavenny and four other like-ships were escorted from Portsmouth by a naval frigate, the HMS Weymouth.

Fierce storms in the English Channel forced the convoy to split up and the Abergavenny sailed into Portland Roads, waiting until the storms had died down so that it could resume the journey. While waiting for help with navigating the dangerous interior waters, the ship hit the Shambles, which caused a lot of damage to the hull. Too slowly, a single life boat was manned and released, but never seen again. This minimal response to the problems seem to be because the captain was quite slow to understand just how dire the situation was and there were no other life boats loaded and released until the ship's long boat floated free and some of the crew and troops jumped in and are said to have survived. But the broken ship did not reach Weymouth beach; the hull was too damaged and sank in Weymouth Bay. The only part of it left above water, the masts, were used by over 140 passengers to keep afloat, but the freezing water and rough conditions meant at least 260 crew and remaining passengers died while waiting to be rescued. Sadly, there were three Weymouth vessels that did come out to help, but reports of the time stated that the boats never came alongside, their men claiming that there were so many people to be saved, their boats would be swamped. Sadly, many felt that the reason those boatmen had not helped was because they were there for the cargo, not the people. As luck would have it, though, a sloop, whose sailors had heard the people on board yelling for help, did come to the rescue and about sixty passengers were saved because of their valiant efforts.

The national newspapers picked up on this story in part because of the fame of its captain. The master of the Earl of Abergavenny was Captain John Wordsworth, brother of one of Britain's most famous 19th century poets, William Wordsworth. John had refused to leave his post as the ship sank and went down with his ship; his body was recovered and he was buried in the cemetery of Wyke Regis' All Saints Church, as were about 100 of the others who also lost their lives in the shipwreck. The others were buried in Radipole's St.

Ann's Church cemetery. John Wordsworth's sword was eventually recovered from the wreck and returned to his family.

IN MEMORY OF MY BROTHER, JOHN WORDSWORTH, COMMANDER OF THE E. I. COMPANY'S SHIP

THE EARL OF ABERGAVENNY IN WHICH HE PERISHED BY CALAMITOUS SHIPWRECK, FEB. 6, 1805.

Full soon in sorrow did I weep,

Taught that the mutual hope was dust,

In sorrow, but for higher trust,

How miserably deep!

All vanished in a single word,

A breath, a sound, and scarcely heard:

Sea--Ship--drowned--Shipwreck--so it came,

The meek, the brave, the good, was gone;

He who had been our living John

Was nothing but a name. From the **Elegiac Stanzas** by William Wordsworth

The Earl of Abergavenny was the finest of all the East Indiamen making the journeys between Britain and the East. It was built in 1789 for just that purpose and had made seven of those trips before its final voyage. Besides the identity of its captain, the other reason this shipwreck was found in all the national newspapers and magazines was because it was carrying valuable cargo, to include silver coin and £20,000 worth of *private cargo* that Captain Wordsworth had bought with his own and family money in an attempt to make up for previous losses. He was hoping to make a small fortune so that he could retire from the sea and he also wanted to buy a home and to be able to support his poet brother, so that he could devote his life to his art. Fortunately, the cargo was insured and the family got its money back, but the Wordsworth family never recovered from the loss of John.

The cargo from the ship was so valuable that the East India Company did not just leave it at that. In 1805, the same year of the wreck, they hired a man called Tomkin to go down to try to salvage anything he could find, but he was unable to move the heavy, broken timbers of the ship and brought up only bits and pieces. Trying again, a well-known salvage man, or *salvor*, John Braithwaite, was hired and he had much better luck, in part because he used a diving bell, a surprisingly old idea, first employed in ship salvaging attempts in the early 18th century. As he began to find the valuables hidden in the Weymouth wreck, the press covered his progress with interest, as did all of Britain. The salvor brought up silver coins in their original chests worth £75,000, £2.5 million in today's money.

Dreadful hurricane...

In 1815, the East India Company suffered another loss when a whole fleet of its ships were sailing to London from India and once again, extremely windy weather slammed into them and hurled one of the ships onto the Chesil on the Wyke Regis side. There seems to have been a conspiracy of silence regarding this wreck, not unusual for locals accustomed to relieving wrecked ships of their goods, as there is no report as to what happened to the goods that had been on board the ruined ship. The loss of life was terrible, with at least 150 dead, washed up along the local shoreline, from Wyke to Abbotsbury. Most of those were also buried at All Saints Church. In what the vicar of the same church called a *dreadful hurricane*, three other East India ships were also lost in 1824, in the same storm that destroyed Weymouth's esplanade, as well as most of the pier. The grand houses along the seafront were flooded and further up the coast, most of the village of Fleet was washed away. There were also another fifteen ships wrecked all along the Dorset coast. And as ever, most and sometimes all, of the crew and passengers died as their ships broke apart.

Rum, brandy and gin...

The decade of the 1870s was another period of time when there were some dramatic and deadly shipwrecks along the Dorset coast; some of these again put the local communities into the national spotlight, but not always for the right reasons. As in decades and centuries before, the news was focused on the aftermath of the accidents.

The Royal Adelaide was a 1500-tonne fast sailing ship; in 1872, it was moored in the London docks, loading a large cargo which included a lot of rum, brandy and gin. There were 35 passengers who were immigrating to Australia, where those passengers planned to start new lives, along with a crew of 32. Its master, Captain I. Hunter, was very experienced and had made the trip to and from Sydney many times. As the ship made its way to Portland on the night of November 24th, it was sighted as it passed the Portland lighthouse, but the observers noted that it was sailing too close to the rocks. The winds were high that evening and as they worsened, the captain decided to try to shelter at Portland Roads, but the wind sent the ship completely off course, ending up pushing it all the way to West Bay, where it continued to be driven closer and closer to Chesil Beach. The coastguard had been watching the ship as it struggled and lit warning lights on high points along Chesil, all the way to Portland as the ship had been pushed back by the raging sea and headed back to that part of Chesil.

News spread, as with earlier wrecks, and people flocked to watch the fate of the ship and its passengers, to include a Weymouth man, Mr Hamilton Williams, who with other Weymouthites, caught the train to Portland, to join the many spectators. He wrote about the event and sent his account to the popular national magazine The Illustrated London

News a month after the wreck and his article provides an eyewitness account of the incident and it also describes some fairly new inventions being employed by the British coastguard:

> *Far to the leeward we could occasionally discern a glimmering light, and we set off in its direction along the beach as fast as we could run. Presently a blue light flashed up from the vessel, whose outline we could just see blurred and dim through sand. Almost as we came opposite her she drifted broadside on the beach, despite her anchors, which found no holding ground. Fearfully she heaved and rolled in the aweful sea. It seemed as if the delivering rocket was never going off on its message of help; but at last, straight as an arrow, away it sped right through the rigging of the helpless vessel (It had been fired by the Wyke Rocket Brigade). The cradle was rigged and the coastguard worked like more than men. The passengers and crew were hauled ashore. Through the boiling sea came one after another, grasped ere long they reached the shore by the friendly arm of some stout seaman. Then we began to learn that they had women and children on board, and the fear that the ship might break up before all were saved grew more and more intense. The first mate had already been drowned, madly trying to jump unaided from the ship. A woman too was drowned, falling overboard.*

> *Soon with an aweful lurch to seaward, the mainmast went by the board, the mizzen topmast having already gone. In a few minutes it was seen that the ship had split right in two, a little abaft <in or behind the stern> of the mainmast. Once commenced the work of destruction was not long, though still the cradle was going to and fro, and still there remained others to be saved. These were all congregated astern; and when the last two or three were already in the cradle, about to try their fate when the rope broke, they fell into the cruel surf and were seen no more.*

> *Then we left the shore seeing the ship a hopeless mass of shattered wood; and I do not think that any of us there will ever forget the impression made on us by the wreck of the Royal Adelaide.*

The report includes mention of the *delivering rocket, Wyke Rocket Brigade* and the *cradle* being used by the coastguard who were trying to rescue the Adelaide's passengers and crew. Prior to 1815, the only agency responsible for assisting with shipwrecks was the customs service; in 1815, the Preventative Waterguard, which had been established in 1809 and was the precursor to the coastguard, became involved in experiments with a device that looked a little like a cannon, but when it was set off, it carried a large *delivering rocket* with a rope attached. The rocket was fired at a floundering ship and was supposed to embed itself into the wooden hull, creating a tie between the men at shore and the ship and its passengers.

The "cradle" was then attached to the rope and sent to the ship, to allow passengers to be loaded into the cradle or basket, and pulled to shore.

The first attempt by the Wyke Regis' own Rocket Brigade, whose primary purpose was to help out at shipwrecks with their rockets, failed and it appears the passengers were too afraid to get into the cradle when the second attempt was a success and seemed to have imbedded itself to the hull. Seeing he had a problem, Captain Hunter decided to be the first to leave the ship, hoping he would show it could be done. Sadly, the very last to get into the cradle were a father and son, who were thrown into the sea when the cradle broke apart.

But alas! poor souls, they drank too deep

Of the brandy and rum – then soon fell asleep

In the wind and the rain, to lie all night,

In a drunken state and an aweful plight   by a Portland Poet

As with so many other shipwrecks, the Royal Adelaide was not spared the wreckers; with an estimated 3,000 onlookers, it must have been an incredible sight and a situation even the most determined coastguards could only observe, as once all who could be saved had been, the cargo of the ship began to be washed onto Chesil's shore and the actions of the crowd chased off the officials who tried, but failed, to collect that cargo because they were *greatly intimidated by the naked aggression and violence of the looters* . The Receiver, who was a customs officer, did try to collect as many of the goods as possible, bringing in local militiamen to help keep the crowd at bay and to collect the washed up cargo, but he took little away from the sight. What the local police and militia did carry away were some of the amateur wreckers who got caught red handed and were charged for their attempted crimes.

There was livestock on board the ship, though only one pig made it off alive, swimming to the shore only to be scooped up by one of the many waiting to carry off anything they could. As other things came onto the beach, people fought over who would have them, but then the bottles of gin and the caskets of brandy began to make their way onto the shore and that is when all hell broke loose. The more serious wreckers were taking foolish chances by going into the heavy surf to grab caskets, running off with as many as they could carry, but many others had little or no experience at wrecking and were there out of curiosity; when the spirits began to wash ashore, some of them grabbed at the chance to turn the dramatic and terribly sad event into a macabre party of sorts. In fact, twice as many spectators as passengers died the night of the wreck; those amateur wreckers got so drunk right there on sight, that excess alcohol and exposure killed them: after having drunk so much, many fell asleep on the beach and never woke again.

From excessive drinking

The list of those who were caught by the police for trying to carry off goods from the ship and those who died from drink that night is a surprising one. A local Wyke businessman and his daughter were arrested for concealing a large quantity of handkerchiefs in an attempt to carry them off. The Wyke baker and grocer was caught, along with his daughter, for trying to take off with unnamed goods and another Wyke villager was stopped and found to have small bundles of pound notes hidden under his clothes. All were tried and fined, but many locals did get away with their ill-gotten goods. At various inquests around the community, the courts declared the reasons for the deaths that night: at the inquest held at the Royal Victoria Inn at Ferry Bridge it was *Death from excessive drinking and exposure to the cold*. At an inquest at Cove Inn in the Portland village of Chesil, Weymouth cabinetmaker Thomas Strange and his friend George Gilbert were found to have *Died from exposure to cold, and from having taken an excessive quantity of raw spirits*.

Leaving Britain...

More Britons emigrated away from the British Isles than all European immigrants together during the 19th century and the majority of those, in their hundreds of thousands, sailed to Australia and New Zealand. The journey was usually arduous and required those emigrants to travel 13,000 miles on ships that were ill-equipped for human habitation. But the biggest problems, beyond the lack of sanitation, comfortable accommodation, and decent food, were storms, illnesses, icebergs and worst of all, shipwrecks. As demonstrated by the fate of the Royal Adelaide and so many others, ships bound for distant countries were always at risk of shipwrecks and these were not always something encountered in faraway seas, they could happen very close to home. Another 1870s catastrophe illustrates that point.

The 1210-tonne iron sailing ship the Avalanche was built by an English company, Shaw Savill & Co., who wanted to be the chief provider of passage to New Zealand, a role they fulfilled from 1858 to 1983. This was the company's third purpose-built ship which between 1874 and 1877 had made three successful journeys to Wellington, loaded with both emigrants and cargo. In preparation for its fourth trip, the Avalanche was loaded at the

London docks in September 1877, with 63 passengers and many supplies. As it made its way toward the Dorset coast in September, the ship hit terrible weather approaching Portland, with driving rain and a howling gale. Coming toward the Avalanche, a Canadian ship, the Forest, which had a crew of 21 men and was on its way back to North America, saw the Avalanche's light; the captain of the Forest lit a warning light to be sure the other ship saw his, but it was too late and the Forest, which was a wooden ship, rammed into the middle of the Avalanche, then the Forest was hit by a huge wave and bounced back, ramming the other ship again, just about cutting the larger ship in two.

The passengers, more than half of them women, were asleep and drowned; only three of the crew were able to jump ship, scrambling onto the Forest. But that ship was also in bad shape and the captain, with difficulty, got his boats into the water, with one washed away by a big wave; the second boat was loaded with crew, but drifted off, found much later, but without its passengers. The third boat carried the remaining crew, to include the captain, toward Chesil Beach, but it was clearly struggling and could not land. Two of Portland's famed fishing boats, the lerrets, and their crews, braved the terrible weather at dawn and managed to bring to shore twelve survivors; they were treated with great care and taken to the Seamen's Home in Weymouth.

The Coroner on opening remarked on the gallant deed of the Portland fishermen and thanked them.

Liverpool Journal, September 22, 1877

The fishermen's bravery was recognized and rewarded with a cash award and a lot of positive press for their actions. This was a nice change from the frequent bad press locals had received over the years because of wrecking.

Teetotal...

Not long after the wreck of the Avalanche and Forest, the Board of Trade held an inquest in London, where the third mate and Captain Lockhart of the Forest gave evidence. Their details were identical and when questioned about his competency, the captain claimed that he *carried no intoxicating liquor*, his vessel was *teetotal*, and that this was his first accident in 16 years. In spite of that, the reporters and others listening to the inquest concluded that the whole incident was his fault. In the end, however, he was not punished for the accident.

Parish authorities

As the bodies from the double wreck of the Avalanche and the Forest began to wash up along local beaches, the parish authorities were responsible for collecting and burying them, which they did quickly and with little ceremony. When word got out about this practical but cold hearted treatment of victims of such a sad accident, friends, family and members of the public got together to build a permanent monument. They did this by erecting a small church in Portland's Southwell village, a memorial to the victims; St. Andrews, more commonly referred to by locals as Avalanche Church, overlooked the site of the wreck and opened for services in 1879.

The Devil's Device

A young man called Robert Whitehead, born in Lancashire in 1823, was from a middle class family involved with engineering. Robert was well-educated and became an engineer and designer. He pursued his career first in Italy, in the cloth industry, but not long after moving to Italy, the engineer found himself in the middle of the war between Austria and Italy which broke out in the late 1840s. This was a time when Italy was being torn apart by political divides and the Austrian Empire was claiming ownership of various parts of that fractured country. Robert was then asked to take on a huge public engineering project by the Austrians and he ended up working for an engineering firm in Fiume, where he did very well. Then he was asked by the Austrian navy to construct an armour plated screw frigate, better known to history as an iron clad. It was not a brand new idea to try to make war ships battle proof, but each country building them had their own designs. Robert's, the Ferdinand Maximillian, better known as the Ferdinand Max, was not the best of them, France and England had better designs, but his engines were more reliable than the other countries' models. These ships are often referred to as the invention that moved naval warfare away from three-decked ships with wooden sides to ships with a single deck of heavy guns firing on the broadside. This was the first real step to moving away from wind power to engines, because the new ships did not rely on the weather in order to fight naval battles. It was also the beginning of the industrialisation of warfare on what would become a grand scale.

But for the Whitehead (torpedo), the submarine would remain an interesting toy and but little more.

Admiral HJ May, Royal Naval College, Greenwich, 1906

No one man has cost the world so much by an invention as did the late Mr. Whitehead of Fiume.

Commander E. Hamilton Currey, 1910, author of Sea-Wolves of the Mediterranean, the Grand Period of the

Moslem Corsairs

The improvement in naval engineering brought a new rush to invent bigger and better weapons. While Robert was building engines and ships, an officer of the Austrian Marine Artillery scribbled a rough design of a tiny wooden boat that could be loaded with explosives and somehow used to blow up blockading warships. Another officer, an Italian, built a small, rough model of a similar design, but with a clockwork motor and a pistol-like detonating device. The theory was that the tiny boat would hit a ship, the pistol would detonate the charge and, boom, the ship would sink. The Italian navy was not interested, but as the officer lived near Robert's factory, he took the idea to the engineer who was very interested. This was in 1864. After giving it some consideration, Robert decided that in order for the tiny boat to work, it would have to travel *under* water or it would be too easy to detect. The torpedo, or as many came to call it, the *devil's device*, was born.

As Robert continued to try to perfect his torpedo design, the winds of war were blowing across Europe again and in 1866, war between Prussia and Austria erupted; Italy, which had lost to Austria in the earlier conflict, decided to join in, in hopes Austria would be preoccupied enough that they could get out from under Italian rule. The Austrian navy, thanks to Robert's superior marine engines, won the conflict when it came up against the Italian navy; the victorious admiral wrote to Robert and credited him with the win. Newspapers got wind of the Englishman's part in it all and he suddenly became a public figure. In spite of Italy's loss, they did manage to win their freedom from Austria, but this did not stop Robert from trying to sell his new weapon to the Austrians, but after a lot of testing, it simply did not work. In spite of the setback, he kept selling his other designs for marine engines and his wealth and fame brought him into the highest social circles of Austria; he was even made a Baron for his services to Austrian engineering.

In spite of his successes, the torpedo remained a problem he could not solve until Robert designed a depth-keeping device – which kept the torpedo consistently under water, rather than bobbing in and out of it, a serious fault with the early models – and he called this device 'the secret' because he decided not to patent it in case of pirating.

By the time the torpedo was perfected, the Austrian government was just about broke, but they still bought the weapon. The good news was that they could not afford many, which meant no contract; this allowed Robert to sell to anyone else he could, but once again, there were problems. By the time the weapon was ready, *torpedo,* which is the name of a fish that stuns its victims with electric shock, had become a generic term for any underwater weapon, making his seem quite "common," but there was also the issue of price: Robert wanted £20,000 pounds each of them.

Undaunted, the engineer persevered and used his influence in naval circles to convince the British and American navies to come to his factory in Italy to discuss the weapon. The Americans balked at the price, but the British invited Robert to come home and build a factory in England, the first in Woolwich, where he continued to improve the weapon. At the same time, the price, by the early 1870s, was down to £300 a torpedo and by 1873, orders were pouring in, though there were naval experts who felt this was definitely not good news. There was a mad rush, from countries around the world, to stock up on torpedoes. The world's first arms race was on.

By the mid-to late 1870s, Robert's factories were equipping countries around the world to use the torpedo, which was interesting given the device had never been used in any war time situation; stocking up on torpedoes was speculative buying, a kind of craze. Through the 1880s, there were ups and downs, but Robert's son-in-law, former Austrian naval officer Count Georg Hoyos, who had married Alice Whitehead, Robert's daughter, had created a sister company which meant they needed a new factory. The decision was made to build the new facility in Wyke Regis, and that became known simply as "the Weymouth factory." The location was ideal for its strategic coastal position, abundant stone and fresh water from numerous wells, as well as the excellent harbour and easy access to Europe. The English officer responsible for the British navy buying their newest version of the torpedo, Captain Edwin Gallwey, resigned his commission and moved to Weymouth to become the new factory's manager.

Alice Whitehead wrote a letter to a family member discussing the new site: *Georg says the*

> **Was the Whitehead torpedo the first?**
>
> As with the unnamed Austrian officer, others had had ideas about underwater weapons, going as far back as the 16th century. A man called Conrelius van Drebbel, who may have seen an earlier design drawn by Leonardo da Vinci, was one of the first to try to build a torpedo-like device. This was not successful, but an American called David Bushell, who some American historians refer to as the Father of the Torpedo and mining warfare, built an egg shaped underwater boat whose sole purpose was to deliver explosives to an enemy ship; these boats were not considered weapons themselves, as they were manned and the operator had to go through some complex steps in order to "stick" the explosives to the enemy boat and then move quickly away. Bushell called his invention "The Turtle," which was used during the American Revolution, but it was not particularly successful.

Weymouth business is certain to succeed and the expenses are far lower than he expected. £50,000 will cover all, machines included, and the place will be as big, as useful, and as important as the Fiume one. Fiume was referring to the Italian factory, which was an impressive site, meaning the Weymouth facility was also quite impressive. As well as many buildings, it also included a 1,000-yard pier built out into Portland harbour for test-firing the torpedoes.

Many of Robert's family moved to Weymouth and he built the "villa Whitehead," which overlooked the factory, along with rows of houses for some of his workers, and a private railway to supply the various areas of the facility. The factory took a sleepy, rural part of Weymouth with a small population of mostly fishermen and their families, a small candle factory and farm land to a sprawling mix of industry, which in turn attracted more and more people and which meant more and more building. In 1897, the Whitehead Company built Wyke Regis' first two schools, something that had become necessary because of the huge increase in the population around the factory. Also because of the location and expertise of Whiteheads', the Royal Navy chose Portland for its anti-submarine and torpedo centre, which was active during both world wars.

Love and the Submarine

Never one to miss out on an opportunity, Robert recognized the value of the design of a new warship that was specifically designed to carry and deliver torpedoes: the submarine. His factories soon began to work on building submarines along with torpedoes. Although this production began just after the turn of the 20th century, it is crucial to the understanding of warfare during that century. The first two Whitehead submarines, intended for the Austrian navy, were completed in 1908 and they were simply called U-5 and U-6. Considering how early these submarines were, they were remarkably efficient. They carried three torpedoes each which could be submerged in three and a half minutes. Strangely, it is these early Whitehead submarines that are responsible for the love story that was the basis of one of the 20th century's most popular musicals.

In 1908, the Austrian navy assigned an intelligent young officer to the Whitehead factory in Weymouth to study the design and construction of submarines and torpedoes up close. Although Robert Whitehead had died six years earlier, the family was still in Weymouth, to include Robert's granddaughter Agathe. She could not help but notice the handsome Austrian officer whose name was Kapitanleutnant Georg Ritter von Trapp and the two became inseparable. Agathe was chosen to christen submarine U-5, with Georg at her side and he was eventually made captain of that submarine; the couple married in 1911. They had five children and were very much in love, but when Austria lost its coast during WWI to Italy and Yugoslavia, the captain found himself out of work. Then, in 1922, Agathe died during the diphtheria epidemic sweeping across Europe; she was 32. He hired a nanny for the children and eventually married her. The story was immortalized in the musical of the 1960s, The Sound of Music.

Weymouth's Old Bank

From the 1870s on, the world of British banking grew not just at home, but all over the world, with British bankers doing business in all corners of the globe. But because of downturns in various international markets, bad decisions on the parts of many banks and other issues that are still not completely clear to banking historians, by the 1890s, bank after bank either collapsed or was so near, it had to be bailed out by the Bank of England. In the 1890s, there were major financial crises in almost every region in which British multinational banks operated. This was made worse by the fact that there were no central banks or lenders at the time and many British and British-owned banks worked more or less in a vacuum, meaning there was little or no chance of a bail out for a desperate independent. For instance, in South Africa, beginning in 1889, there was a financial panic caused by goldmine speculators and most local banks there collapsed.

In 1890, London's leading merchant bank, Barings, all but collapsed because it was overly invested in Latin America, where problem after problem meant individuals and companies reneged on the loans Barings had given them. The company was saved by the Bank of England, but these and other issues led to a general loss of faith even in the Bank of England, in part because people thought it unfair that the taxpayer should have to bail out privately owned businesses. Then in 1893, Australia experienced its own bank disasters, when 54 out of its 64 banks closed over a two-year period. Thirty-four of those never reopened. The same or similar problems also hit Asian and New Zealand banks owned by British companies. When the US began to experience serious financial issues, many of which were caused by policies regarding the silver standard, the value of which had collapsed, the whole world was experiencing varying levels of banking disasters. The depression of the 1890s was on and Weymouth and its neighbours were not immune.

Although there were other banks in Weymouth, the biggest, Weymouth Old Bank, which was founded in the late 18th century and had become the most important financial institution in the area, held most of the town's prominent businesses accounts. These included utility companies, Weymouth College, Cosens and Company, along with many others. The bank had done very well for many decades, with branches not just in Weymouth, but Bournemouth, Portland and Dorchester, but after the deaths of the founders, who had left it to sons and a nephew, it increasingly made poor investment decisions as well as sold off many of the bank's assets. By the time fearful customers - who had heard of the bank's problems because a circular that had been mailed to them informing them that all payments out had been suspended - gathered outside of the Weymouth branch on St. Thomas Street in March 1897, the bank's liabilities were up to £500,000, which in today's money is just under £29,000,000. Because the primary directors of the bank were well-respected men, to include two mayors of Weymouth and Dorchester, a justice of the peace, and others who held or who had held prominent positions, many customers believed the directors would be able to turn the problems around, in spite of the fact that the quarry owners who banked at the Portland branch were worried they could not meet the quarrymen's payrolls and many who had trusted their small but much needed savings to the bank were fearful of losing their life savings. But the faith was unfounded, as the press began to explore the true nature of the bank's terrible business practices under the "new" directors who had inherited their positions and a formal audit of the bank revealed just how corrupt – and inept – its leadership had been, going back years prior to its final death knell in 1897.

Hopeful customers continued to believe that the measures taken to recoup some of the funds by seizing the properties of the directors, who had taken monies out, made risky investments in Britain and around the world, and spent lavishly on homes and luxury goods, would mean they would get their money back. However, the sale of the banks' properties did not raise anything like the monies owed to former customers; six years after the crash, they received only pennies on the pound of their savings. What was once Weymouth's most successful bank was eventually torn down to build a supermarket.

God Save the Queen

The same year Weymouth's Old Bank failed, all across Britain her subjects helped Queen Victoria celebrate her Diamond Jubilee, her sixtieth year on the throne. The first royal jubilees began with her grandfather, King George III, when he celebrated his Golden Jubilee in 1809, after fifty years on the throne. Dorset's celebrations held in honour of both monarchs, especially Weymouth's, were varied, from the statues erected for both, but especially for Queen Victoria. The statue erected in her honour, as well as the Jubilee clock on the seafront, were just part of it. There were special church services, processions, band concerts, luncheons for entire villages, fetes, teas, fireworks, and though they were a few years late with it, Portland planned its Victoria Gardens for the Jubilee, though it was not opened until 1904. Some of the villages even paid for their workhouse inmates to enjoy a celebratory dinner.

Public Lavatory

Not everyone was a fan of Weymouth's tribute to Victoria, the grand clock on the seafront. In his 1922 **The Soil of Dorset**, the wonderfully named author of that book, F.J. Harvey Darton, had this to say about Weymouth: *What I complain of at Weymouth is not its prosperity or its efficiency, but the desperate ugliness, even sordidness of everything modern in it. Even the bridge is mean. The newer buildings have not so much as the credit of vulgarity on the grand scale. The amazing Jubilee clock is symbolical. It is of iron painted green and yellow, in the Public Lavatory Style, with a sort of bas-relief of Victoria on each of its sides.*

Darton was referring to the bridge that connected Melcombe Regis with old Weymouth and he may have thought it ugly, but the history of Weymouth's bridges is a long and sometimes-controversial one and some of its bridges were quite handsome. The two sides had squabbled over water and port rights between them for hundreds of years, so much so that Queen Elizabeth got involved; in 1570 her appointed commissioners advised the two towns be connected. The fighting between the two continued until the first bridge was built, out of wood, in 1597. That bridge was supported by wooden piles, with seventeen arches and a central drawbridge. This connected the two towns, where prior, the only way to go over the water to either side was to take a small boat that was pulled from side to side by rope, called the Leland's ferry, a service that began in 1533. Then a Charter of James I in 1601 made the union of the two sides fairly successful and the two began to work together rather than in constant opposition.

The original bridge was badly damaged during the English Civil War and the wood used for repair came from the New Forest. Because maritime business was booming by the second half of the 18th century, there was a need for a bigger and better bridge and a new one was donated in 1770 by a former MP, John Tucker, who had served Weymouth and Melcombe Regis in Parliament from 1727 to 1737, as well as serving as mayor of Weymouth in the years 1726, 1732, 1738, 1754, 1763 and 1772. The new bridge was seventy yards long and provided much more space for the ever-increasing trading going on at the harbour; but, as harbour business just became busier and busier, another new bridge was planned on the same site. This was completed in 1824 and was built of stone and allowed for larger ships to go in and out of the harbour's backwater. It was made even larger in 1885.

Another important bridge, the Westham bridge, was built in the latter 1850s, which made it much easier to pass over the backwater; it was made of wood and for twenty years cost a halfpenny toll to cross.

At least as important as the other Weymouth bridges was the Smallmouth Bridge. The first one that crossed over the water running between the Fleet and the harbour at the point where Wyke Regis and the Portland causeway meet was built in 1839; prior to that, the only way to cross was to take the ferry, which had operated over centuries and was precarious at best during stormy weather. The impetus to build the bridge was the terrible storm of 1824, which among other disasters to include the almost-complete devastation of the village of Fleet, destroyed the ferry and killed the ferryman, but it still took all those years to see it built. The bridge was six hundred feet long, twenty feet wide and was built on piles, high enough not to be swamped by the tides. The charge for passage over the bridge was one and a half pence and other traffic, like horses and carriages, had to be weighed to determine the charge. The alternative, which was popular with tourists, was to wait until the tide was low in order to cross on the sand of the small bay and onto the beach on the other side.

Dorset Dialect

Where the bridge out at Woodley did stride,
Wi' his wide arches' cool sheäded bow,
Up above the clear brook that did slide
By the poppies, befoam'd white as snow;
As the gilcups did quiver among
The white deäsies, a-spread in a sheet.
There a quick-trippèn maïd come along,
Aye, a girl wi' her light-steppèn veet.

From William Barnes' **The Love Child**

Born in 1801, Dorset clergyman William Barnes is credited with preserving and making popular the dialect of the county; he was born on a farm outside of Sturminster Newton and became a clergyman after graduating with a degree in divinity from Cambridge. Although he served the church from 1848 until his death in 1886 at the small churches of Whitcombe and Winterbourne Came, he was also a mathematician, poet and philologist. The last two came together when he wrote not just the most famous poetry of Dorset, but of its time; his work is said to have paved the way for writers like Thomas Hardy, who was tutored by Barnes, to embrace writing based on local life and legend. That is because being a philologist, the poet in Barnes recognized the beauty of writing in local dialect, which he also explored and wrote about in a number of books on philology.

Barnes was not alone in his love of the dialogue of the West Country. The Philological Society was founded in 1842 in London and there were members who wrote many treatises and full length books about various counties' dialects. In one of those books, written in 1864, members of the society brought together a number of theories about the origins of British dialects, with a special focus on Dorset. They declared that it had been influenced by many languages, to include Anglo-Saxon, "Gothic," Icelandic, German (differentiating it from Anglo-Saxon), Dutch and a number of others.

Some of the words they identified are not too difficult for the modern ear to make sense of, as they are still, in some way, familiar; words like *afeard*- afraid – are a good example. But there are many others that are either completely "foreign" or are somehow familiar, but mean something very different now than they did in the 19th century and many centuries before. Some of these words provide a glimpse into the world of, for instance, haymaking,

For many centuries, Weymouth and its neighbours' surrounding fields have been planted with a variety of crops, to include hay, and that is so today. But conversations about the process of haymaking would have been difficult for the modern ear to make any sense of. When *haỹmeäken*, *Zwath* (grass) was *tedded* (thrown into piles) and then it was raked into *rollers* (little ridges) and sometimes piled into *cocks* (heaps). The following day, the *zwath* was piled into *passels* (parcels/larger piles) and in the late afternoon, these were put into *weäls* and those were *pooked* (put into yet larger piles). The *Haỹward*, on the other hand, had nothing to do with *haymeaken*, he was the warden of the local common whose primary job was to assure that only people with the right to graze their animals on the common were doing so. And then there was the language of food: I'll have a *smatch* (taste) of that *quob* (jiggly) jelly and *rean* (eat it greedily)!

The dialect still in use but comes from many centuries past includes ramshackle (rickety), put up wi (bear patiently), put up (take bed or board), handy, harness, nettle (to pique), niggle (to complain of trifles), nudge, peärt (lively), peaked (thin), pitch (throw hay on a wagon), whack (a smart blow), whopper (a lie), wrag (scold), well-to-do (living in easy circumstances), scuff (drag shoe on ground), shirk (to evade), slim (slender), stop-gap (fill in for something out of necessity), tramp (vagabond), rundown (depreciate, speak ill of, find fault with), skew-whiff (distorted), week's end (Saturday night), wet (light rain) and middling (far from handsome).

A Glossary

There are many wonderful words that have fallen out of use today, but would have been part of the daily vocabulary of local people through to the beginning of the 20th century. Some of these were used elsewhere and some only in Dorset. Those include:

anby = soon

annan = what did you say?

a-stogg'd = feet stuck in the mud

ballywrag = accuse or scold using bad language

beëns = because

caddle = perplexity

choke dog = a funny reference to Dorset's hard cheese

chop = barter or exchange

crandy = merrymaking

daps = exact likeness

de-da = simple or foolish

ditter = a children's game

drabble-tail = the dirty back hem of a dress

drawlatchet = walking slowly

dringe = squeeze or push

drong = narrow passageway

dunch = deaf

eve = condensation

fenēg = not to answer a call of duty

footy = insignificant

gally = to frighten

gee = get on well together

glene = snear

good-now = do you know or you must know

gwoad = a fifteen-foot measurement

halsen = to forebode evil

heart = discouraged

highlows = high shoes

mixen = dung heap

mould = the skull

nang = a great insult

ne-na = foolish

nirrup = donkey

nunnywatch = a quandary

peck upon = dominate   pillem = dust

pure = quite well (How are ye? Pure!)

quaddle = to make limp or flabby

quar = stone quarry

rea'nban = have an opinion

reremouse = bat

ride = angry when teased

rig = uncastrated horse that is not perfect

sar = feed animals

scammish = awkward

scram = distorted

screed = to shun

scute = to reward or pay (strictly W. Dorset use)

shark = sneak off

shrovy = begging at Shrovetide or confessing

skillen = a shed

slack-twisted = inactive, no energy

slommocken = dirty or slatternly

snap pin tongs = game of musical chairs

snoatch = breathe through the nose

so'tpoll = in broader English dialect, this meant a silly person, but locally, it meant someone of weak mind

sock = sigh loudly

sooner = ghost or spirit

sprēthe = chapped as in 'My lips a-sprēthed.'

squail = throw stones

steän = lay with stones

stunpoll = a blockhead

swipes = very thin beer

tail-an end = eager to do anything

there-right = immediately

thirtover = perverse or morose

tilty = irritable

tine = kindle a fire

tole = entice or allure

tooty = cry in a low, broken tone

towse = row or uproar (West Dorset only)

treäde = trash or unwholesome food

trig = prop or hold up

trot = foolish talk

turk = a large example of a breed or type 'A turk of a dog'

tut = piece work

twite = reproach

twoad's meat = toadstool

undercreepēn = underhanded or working against another in a sly way

upzies wi' = tit for tat

vang = to earn

veäre = litter of pigs

veze = fidget

vitty = properly, neatly

vlee = fly

vwo'th = exit, way out

werrit = sorry

wevet = cobweb

zennit = seven nights a week

zoundy = swoon

zweal = sing

And possibly the best words in the Dorset dialect? God Almighty's Cow, a lady bird; vearies hearts, Dorset fossils thought to be the heads or hearts of fairies; Dumbledore, the humble bee and Snape (West Dorset only), a spring. J.K. Rowling must know about the local language of earlier centuries.

To close

When I was a student of history, my professors often commented on what it was to be "professional" in our approach to exploring the past, and their teachings included the "fact" that anything which had happened fifty to one-hundred years before was not really history, it was "current events." In the 21st century, we could argue about that philosophy, although it was one I also passed on to my own history students, but there is a real logic to this, especially when researching and writing about local histories, when the writer is exploring the many sources needed to inform a thorough look at what has come before; when we are working with sources from the mid to late 19th through the early 20th century especially, it can be a tricky process. For one, there are so many more resources available than for previous centuries, which is a good thing, but can also mean conflicting information. One newspaper, for instance, may have reported on an event in one way and another may be describing the same event, but the two can contain radically different, and opposing, details.

Then there are personal letters, national journals, royal society papers and on and on, often presenting an event or other historical detail very differently, one from the other, or possibly presenting hearsay or opinion as reality. So, which is correct, if any? In other words, what makes for a credible source? And that is just the tip of the iceberg. Then we have those lovely people whose families may go back generations in the community or communities being examined and have grown up with stories of those places' pasts. Those stories may or may not be accurate, but the same people are often married to them and consider themselves experts on local history; anyone who says otherwise is the bad guy. I have had that experience, as have other historians I have known and have worked with, and it can be difficult to deal with and very frustrating. That said, I have chosen to listen to my sage professors and have ended this 19th century history of Weymouth and its neighbours with the death of the now-second longest reigning monarch in British history.

When Queen Victoria died in 1901, she had been on the throne for sixty-three years and had ruled over one quarter of the world's population. Especially in her earlier years as monarch, when her husband Prince Albert had taken such an active interest in Portland harbour's huge building projects, it made the royal couple an important part of local history and her life was coming to its end at an interesting juncture in the local story, given the amazing events that began to take place in the late 19th and into the 20th century.

By the 1870s, many Dorset towns and villages had benefitted from the requirement that local government take responsibility for public health by creating sanitary authorities, but those were replaced in 1894 when the Local Government Act required the creation of rural and urban districts, which were responsible for public health matters like the provision of clean drinking water, sewers, street cleaning and slum clearance. This had a profound impact on public health on both the national and local levels; Dorset had dozens of urban and rural sanitary districts.

In Wyke Regis, although Robert Whitehead died very early in the century, the Whitehead torpedo factory prospered and built its own housing stock in order to provide homes for its many workers; over time, schools, pubs and clubs also appeared, in order to service an ever-growing population in what had once been a tiny fishing village and vast farm land. It even had its own railroad that ran through the site, picking up and delivering supplies and the finished products; by the turn of the 20th century, the main rail line which passed right by the factory dropped off and picked up at least one-thousand factory workers a day at the nearby Wyke Halt.

Portland port continued to grow in importance to the Royal Navy and it was here that the first naval aircraft flew for the first time from the deck of a naval vessel as it steamed to the Royal Fleet Review in Weymouth Bay in 1912. By the eve of WWI, there were so many warships in Portland harbour, the Admiralty decided to move them in order to try to prevent a German attack, followed by blocking off parts of the harbour.

The decision was taken to sink an old battleship across the southern entrance to the harbour to try to stop torpedoes and submarines from entering, though there were U-boats in the immediate area throughout the war. The HMS Formidable was sunk just off of Portland Bill by a German submarine, though there were minesweepers based locally that worked constantly to try to keep Weymouth Bay safe. Mid-way through the war, in 1917, Dorset became the focus of the Admiralty's anti-submarine strategy, with a base built on Portland where a lot of the research was done on underwater sound echo-location, the precursor to sonar.

Many men from the local area served in WWI and interestingly, Weymouth was the site chosen to create an Australian command depot in 1915 and after Gallipoli, with its huge casualty rate, there were eventually four Australian Anzac camps in Weymouth, where those casualties who were not expected to be completely well within three months were brought to be treated and to convalesce. Eighty-six of those did not survive and were buried in the Melcombe Regis cemetery.

There was also a large prisoner of war camp built just on the edge of Dorchester in Poundbury, probably the first of its kind in the UK; it housed German prisoners-of-war and eventually had over 4,500 men serving their internment there. There were no reports of violence and the local people accepted and even embraced the German presence. Some of the prisoners worked around the town, gardening in the public gardens and one was even hired by Thomas Hardy to work in his own gardens.

The Weymouth area saw much more wartime activity during WWII than it had during WWI, with tens of thousands of Americans arriving, especially as the preparations for D-Day were being made. Enormous amounts of military equipment made their way to the area, by sea and by road. As one of the major staging harbours of D-Day, Weymouth's causeway and harbour were remarkably busy as the allies prepared to cross the channel to French beaches; those leaving from the local area fought on Omaha Beach and many of the wounded found their way back to Weymouth, as did many of the bodies of those who did not survive the bloody battles.

Dorset was also home once again to German prisoner-of-war camps; they were hidden away in places like Cattistock, West Lulworth, Wimborne Minster, and Portland Dockyard, which served as a transit camp. Thousands arrived into Weymouth harbour, especially as the war was coming to an end. Some of the prisoners stayed in the area, marrying local women and raising families. Other Germans made their way to Weymouth, Portland and their surrounds, but these were the German bombers who targeted the torpedo factory once again, as well as other strategic locations on Portland and around Weymouth.

After the war, many historical buildings that had been damaged by German bombs were levelled rather than restored, all in the name of urban renewal, and the area saw its ups and downs, as it had in so much of its history. The navy continued to be a very important part of local life as a port, especially as host to many NATO ships, to include nuclear submarines, until the 1990s. And also like all other eras in its history, Weymouth and its neighbours continue to adapt to the times.

Author's notes

As with the first volume of <u>The History of Weymouth and its Neighbours</u>, many *many* sources were used to inform this book. Those include local and national newspapers, personal diaries, scholarly journals, military records, magazines, images, government reports and like-sources, Royal Society notes and papers, poetry, dictionaries, surveys, cookbooks, government records, maps, Parliamentary records, old dictionaries, photographs, maps, blue prints, muster and tax rolls and fictional stories.

www.ingramcontent.com/pod-product-compliance
Lightning Source LLC
Chambersburg PA
CBHW081250040426

42452CB00015B/2770